UNDER AN
AFRICAN SKY

First published in 2022 by Puxley Productions Ltd..

Copyright © 2022 by Bill Samuel.

All rights reserved.

No part of this document may be reproduced or transmitted in any form or by any means, electronic, mechanical, photocopying, recording, or otherwise, without prior written permission of the copyright owner.

This is a work of nonfiction. Any similarity between the characters and situations within its pages, and places, persons, or animals living or dead, could be unintentional and co-incidental. Some names and identifying details have been changed or omitted to, in part, protect the privacy of individuals.

The right of Bill Samuel to be identified as the author of this work has been asserted by him in accordance with sections 77 and 78 of the Copyright, Designs and Patents Act, 1988.

British Library Cataloguing in Publication Data.
A catalogue record for this book is available from the British Library.

ISBN: 978-1-916072-7-7 (hardback)

Typeset in Berling
Printed and bound by Ingram Spark in the UK.

Cover Design and typesetting by Jamie Keenan.

Also by Bill Samuel

AN ACCIDENTAL BOOKSELLER

and

AN ACCIDENTAL ENVOY

www.billsamuel.co.uk
@booksellerbill

UNDER AN AFRICAN SKY

My Time in Kenya

BILL SAMUEL

Contents

1. Introduction 1
2. Arrival, in which I see my first ostrich and a small family of snakes 7
3. Family Life, in which we are chased by a buffalo and find a monkey in a cupboard 15
4. The Romance of Audit, in which I buy a beer for the King of Denmark and meet some lions after a dinner party 31
5. The Land, in which a crocodile spoils our lunch and I am nearly killed by a mosquito 53
6. The Mountains, in which I climb Kilimanjaro in purple flares and Italian POWs climb Mount Kenya in prison clothing 63
7. The Coast, in which I see a hammerhead shark on a bicycle and meet a large grouper 79
8. The Middle Years, in which I buy an ashtray for the President and acquire a hotel site on the Nile 91
9. The Characters, in which a friend reveals his Odessa membership and another kicks a lion's bottom 121
10. Round Table, in which I have a close encounter with a hippopotamus and attempt to influence Kenya's foreign policy 131
11. The Closing Years, in which I fly round Kilimanjaro and become a money launderer 141
12. Moving On, in which I say goodbye to Africa and leave by the back door 153
13. An African Family, in which my daughters are bridesmaids at a wedding and I share a barbecued goat with an old freedom fighter 159
14. Later, in which I battle British bureaucracy and avoid being mugged in a Zambian market 175

Swahili glossary

Askari – a guard or watchman. Also an ordinary soldier

Ayah – nanny

Chakula – food

Donga – stony river bed, usually dry but prone to flash floods

Dudu – an insect or creepy crawly. I've heard the word applied to a large lobster

Duka – small local shop, convenience store

Fundi – a craftsman, skilled worker or specialist

Guka (Kikuyu) – grandfather

Kikoi – all-purpose wraparound garment of colourful cotton, at 3' x 5' smaller (and in my view more practical) than a sarong

Makuti – banana-leaf thatch

Matatu – a shared taxi, invariably old and battered and prone to breakdowns.

Murram – laterite, the red earth road surface common in Africa

Mzee – old man, a term of respect.

Panga – a long, broad-bladed knife, an essential implement used for everything from gardening to murder.

Shifta – Somali bandits roaming north-east Kenya

Wapi...? – where is...?

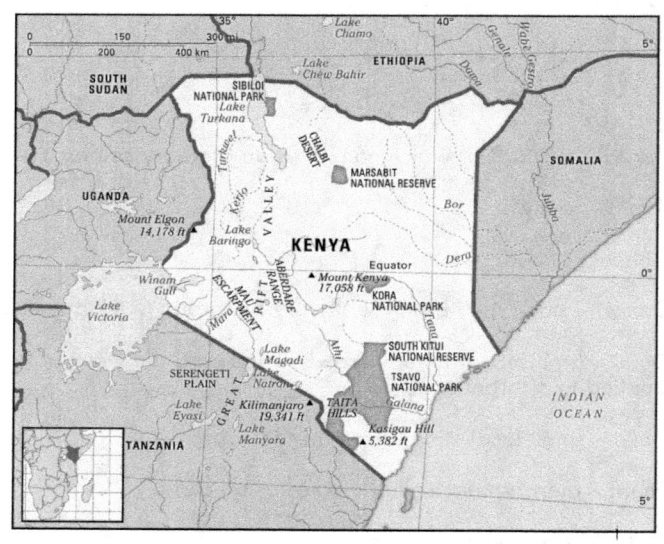

1. INTRODUCTION

I CANNOT ADEQUATELY DESCRIBE THE passion I have for East Africa: for the beauty that reaches right into my soul, the peace I have felt on top of some of its tallest mountains, the rawness of its wildlife, the vibrance of its people. Were I alone in this world I would live in Africa.

While writing *An Accidental Bookseller*, a memoir about my family's business Foyles Bookshop, I realised both how a single memory can bring a whole chain of memories from the dark of the subconscious back into the light, and that some are blurred by the passage of time or sharpened by nostalgia. This is a subjective account of the Africa I knew fifty years ago and I see no need to apologise if it occasionally parts company with objective history. My wife Bente and I went out there on a two-year contract in 1967 and stayed for nine years. We brought up our two older daughters there and enjoyed a magical family life in the sunshine. We worked, we played, we grew, we made friends, we had fun. Memories crowd together, nine years' worth, which I could condense into a few pages or expand into a whole book: the excitement of our first household shop in Bazaar Street; dancing late into the night in our Nairobi living room; trips into the bush with my father-in-law, swimming with him at Buffalo Springs and watching the elephants splashing around just after we left the water; a weekend with my family in the Samburu Game Reserve camping beside a crocodile-infested river, log fire burning high, the beautiful voice of Ella Fitzgerald playing on our primitive cassette player as we danced under a full African moon; the never-failing sense of awe at the dramatic appearance of the Rift Valley as we drove north; drifting over the coral reefs of the Indian Ocean, teeming with brilliantly coloured small fish; standing on top of Mount Kilimanjaro as the sun rose and turned the endless plains of Africa from black to gold.

Africa was where I got to know my daughters as people, as friends. Marina, not yet two when we moved from Copenhagen to Nairobi, took the transition from northern Europe to East Africa in her confident little stride and loved the sunshine and the freedom to spend much of the day outside in a garden full of flowers, *blomster* in Danish, which she rendered as *dumdiyer*. Margaret, now known to all as Maggie but in my heart still Barget or Gog from her early attempts at her own name, was born a year after we arrived. She spent much of her first few months swaddled in brightly coloured wraps on the back of Jeannie, our house girl, whose unique musky smell was so imprinted on Maggie's memory that, forty-five years later when they met again after having had no contact for decades, she spent an entire evening snuggling up to Jeannie, inhaling the perfume of her babyhood. With their Danish ancestry the girls were golden in the sunshine, golden hair and golden skin with that African sunshine reflected in their smiles.

And perhaps most importantly Africa was where I got to know myself. I arrived a twenty-six-year-old accountant used to the slight formality of that profession, fully adult but never having been in a position of real authority or responsibility; I left nine years later with the confidence of an entrepreneur and a wealth of experience, shaped by both success and failure, a risk taker ready to meet the next challenge.

Books have figured large in my life from early childhood onwards. They ignited both my curiosity and my wanderlust. Like many of my generation I started with Enid Blyton and Swallows and Amazons, but the book that most changed my life was the unlikely 'Wings over the Zambezi' by Wilfrid Robertson, which I found in my prep-school library. A less-than-brilliant wartime thriller set in southern Africa, with the stereotypical English goodies and German baddies of the writing of the time, it fired in my curious ten-year-old self a desire to see Africa, to experience parts of the world which were radically different from the comfortable Home Counties of England where I spent my early years. That desire gradually grew, fed by the wildly exotic adventures of Allan Quatermain invented by H. Rider Haggard and the jingoistic historical fiction of G. A. Henty, all planting indelible, albeit inaccurate, pictures in my impressionable young mind.

I nurtured my quiet dreams of Africa through my teenage years, while Harold Macmillan's 'winds of change' blew through the continent and the Empire of my childhood reading was slowly and inevitably dismantled, replaced by brave new nations intent on finding their own identities and establishing themselves free from the apron strings of their European rulers, Kenya prominent among them. I had ambitions to be a civil engineer and travel the world building beautiful bridges with, as my role model, the great nineteenth-century entrepreneur Weetman Pearson, but fate had other ideas. I failed to get to university, a prerequisite for engineering: my route to Africa was through the more mundane world of accountancy.

I qualified as a Chartered Accountant in 1964, having served my articles in London, and we moved to Denmark, the country of my wife's birth. I worked for Price Waterhouse in Copenhagen for two years and would have happily continued to do so, but the strange Danish tax rules imposed on foreigners at the time made staying on for a third year financially deeply unattractive and, being still in my mid-twenties, I was not considered old enough to get a sufficiently challenging job in the UK. However, during the nineteenth century, when the UK dominated world commerce, the London accounting firms led by Price Waterhouse and Peat, Marwick, Mitchell had established networks of offices throughout the world to service their international clients. Chartered accountancy was now a passport to employment almost anywhere; it seemed an ideal time to fulfil my young ambitions and spend a couple of years in Africa. Having a young baby my wife sensibly insisted that we live in a city with adequate medical facilities, so I replied to an advert for an audit post in Nairobi with the local affiliate of Deloitte, Gill and Johnson.

I had a letter from Deloitte by return post asking me to phone and arrange an interview. It was my twenty-sixth birthday the following Sunday, so I flew back to London, spent the weekend with my parents and was interviewed on the Monday. I was asked little about my skills and qualification, only how soon I could start.

I gave my notice to Price Waterhouse, a company for which I had greatly enjoyed working, and headed, finally, for the Dark Continent, which I soon found out was, after Antarctica, the lightest of continents, bathed in sunshine, with even its moonlight somehow brighter and sharper than that of Northern Europe. My childhood dreams were to be realized.

The Kenya I found myself in was a vibrant young developing nation with a multicultural population broadly united in its ambitions for the country. The corruption which has since set much of Africa back decades had not yet reared its ugly head and the government, under the benevolent dictatorship of Jomo Kenyatta, was helping to make things happen. I was determined to play my modest part.

The nine years I was eventually to spend there were nine years of richness, during which life took me beyond the bounds of the accountancy profession and unexpectedly launched me into the wider world of business. I experienced all that I had hoped for from the reading of my childhood, great sweeping landscapes, encounters with wild animals and spear-carrying nomads tending their herds of exotic cattle. I got to know many larger-than-life characters who seemed to fit comfortably into the broad Kenyan landscape but who would have been quite out of place in more developed and settled countries. When I finally returned to the UK I was to find that I too was slightly out of place.

2. ARRIVAL

HOW DO I BEGIN TO explain what it was to move to East Africa in the late 1960s, long before the age of cheap air travel, when few of my compatriots' horizons stretched beyond the borders of Europe?

It was towards the end of the age of the great ocean liners and we had booked to sail with Union-Castle Line from London through the Suez Canal to Mombasa then on to Nairobi by train. The journey would have taken a week or so but a war in the Middle East closed the Canal, plans were changed, and we were forced to fly. This deprived us of the gradual transition from temperate northern Europe to tropical East Africa and from one life to another. Emigrating before the age of air travel took time and imposed real distance, both physical and psychological, between the old home and the new. The abrupt, jolting changes which air travel brings have removed some of the magic of anticipation from the world.

With Bente and twenty-month-old Marina I departed from Heathrow Terminal 3, still known at the time as the Oceanic Terminal. We flew in a VC10, the very latest of airliners, the design of which was heavily influenced by BOAC's requirement for it to operate from short airfields in Africa where both temperatures and altitudes could be high. In addition to the war in the Middle East, civil war was raging in Nigeria, so to avoid all areas of conflict we took a huge dogleg to the east, being routed via Teheran where we stopped to refuel just after dawn. My wife and daughter were sleeping but this was the first time I had left Europe and I was determined to set foot in what I still thought of as Persia, once home to one of the great classical civilizations, to experience the mysterious Orient. I went into the terminal and ordered a coffee, expecting some exotic and spice-laden Eastern brew: what I got was a cup of hot water and a sachet of Nescafé.

Some hours later, at around midday local time on Friday 20th July 1967, we landed at Nairobi's Embakasi Airport, the end of a long journey and the start of my lifelong love affair with Africa. We were met by Ted Johnson, one of the partners of Gill and Johnson, my new employers. G & J had been founded in Nairobi in 1908 by Ted's father and a Mr. Gill, whose son Jim was also a partner. Ted drove us into the city in his Peugeot 404 Estate, at that time the reliable workhorse of East Africa, along the road which skirts the Nairobi Game Park. I sat in the back, entranced, soaking up the unfamiliar landscape and my first acacia thorns: small and scrubby, they were not the majestic yellow-barked giants along the road into Naivasha which later became so familiar, but this was still Africa as I had imagined it. And in among the thorns I saw a solitary ostrich in silhouette, my first glimpse of African wildlife.

We were taken to the Ambassador Hotel on Kenyatta Avenue, Nairobi's beautiful central thoroughfare, designed to be wide enough to turn a full-sized ox-wagon and lined with jacaranda trees which, a few months later, would be little individual clouds of purple blossom. The hotel was very much from the colonial era and, as I later discovered, the chosen venue for the regular monthly lunches of the local Nazi Society. After resting we went down to the hotel restaurant which, as was typical at the time, had a dance floor and resident band: we dined and danced, the three of us together, and slept our first night in Africa, Marina eschewing the cot provided for the security of the small warm space between her parents.

The next morning, I walked the few hundred yards to the office where I was introduced to the youngest partner, David Lloyd Jones, who unhesitatingly lent me his car for the weekend. (We soon learned to treat cars as necessities of life to be lent and borrowed freely, not, as English culture has it, treasured possessions to be guarded and polished and worshipped.) Then we were taken to our new home in the suburb of Westlands.

A boxy ground-floor flat, the lowest of six, it was accessed by a very steep drive, at the bottom of which was a parking area bounded by a couple of large moonflower trees and an embankment of butchered stone supporting the higher parking area of our neighbours. The front door led into a small hallway with a shower room to the left and small single bedroom to the right. Frosted glass doors led into the sitting-dining room, the sitting area heated by a small built-in electric fire, the only heating in the flat. To the right a door led through to the kitchen, and to the left was the door to a double room with the main bathroom en-suite, and another to a second small single bedroom. Half of the external sitting-room wall, behind a retractable security grille, comprised French windows leading to a small balcony with steps down to the beautiful gardens: a flattish lawn which tumbled down a rocky hillside to a fast-running little stream, bordered by towering trees. The far side of the stream was natural forest, home to monkeys who visited regularly and no doubt many other animals who kept their distance. In among the rocks were flowering shrubs, including a number of poinsettias which I had always thought of as house plants coming into their own around Christmas time, but in the more equable climate of East Africa grow to become sizeable bushes. At the end of the block was our integral garage/utility room, its outside wall draped with honeysuckle and inhabited, as we soon discovered, by a family of emerald-green tree snakes, harmless and in their way quite beautiful. As a home it was basic but adequate, lacking the cosy charm of our lovely duplex apartment near Copenhagen: it is a long way from Charlottenlund to Westlands, both literally and metaphorically, but the setting was idyllic and we were to be happy there.

David introduced us to Bazaar Street, an eclectic mix of hardware shops, carpet dealers, spice merchants and tailors run by unctuous Indian shopkeepers at their most stereotypical. It was completely and utterly different to anything I had experienced before. In less than twenty-four hours I had been magically transported from my parents' Berkshire home to the souks of my childhood reading, my flying carpet a BOAC VC10. I felt completely safe; everything was strange and exotic and exciting but at the same time totally unthreatening. Looking back, it was not until well into the twenty-first century that I ever felt the least bit unsafe in central Nairobi. We bought some essentials, returned to our little flat and started our new life, thousands of miles from our families and uncontactable except by letter.

At the flats there was a 'shamba boy', Njoroge, who had been looking after the gardens since the property was built more than thirty years earlier. I soon learnt that domestic servants were always 'boy' or 'girl', a hangover from the recent colonial era which surprisingly didn't seem to cause offence. We were being advised on domestic matters by a work colleague, a matronly lady named Dolly, and although Bente had been adamant that she would never want or need a house servant we were persuaded that it was expected of us as it provided employment. Dolly, through the network of her own domestic servants duly found us a house-girl. She turned up at our flat the next day, shy and speaking little English, and Njoroge contrived subtly to make her life a complete misery. After a couple of days she resigned.

The following morning Njoroge brought along his sixteen-year-old daughter Jane Njeri, fresh out of school, and informed us that she was our new house girl. Jane Njeri had

had a basic education and could read and write; although shy she was obviously intelligent and we were happy to take her on. Unused to the double consonants starting many Kikuyu names we called her Jeannie, and the close relationship we developed with her and her family, about which I shall write in detail later, continues to this day.

We soon discovered that a car each was an absolute essential in Nairobi. In common with most employers G & J offered short-term car loans, enough to buy a new VW Beetle or second-hand Peugeot 404, both tough enough to take the hammering inflicted by Kenya's rough roads. I opted for the former and took delivery of my first new car early in our first week. One of my colleagues was returning to the UK and for a very modest amount we bought his wife's old Austin A30, which served Bente reliably for a number of years although, as we immediately found out, could only manage our very steep drive in reverse gear.

The following weekend Dolly's husband George took us for a drive and for the first time I experienced the full grandeur of the Kenyan landscape. We drove north on what was then the main road leading from Nairobi to Western Kenya, and on to Uganda. The neat stone houses of the Nairobi suburbs gradually gave way to a mix of traditional mud huts thatched with banana leaves and untraditional corrugated iron shacks, with roadside stalls selling fruit and vegetables, sheepskins and wood carvings. There were a few miles of fairly dense forest which abruptly parted to reveal the magnificent sweep of the Rift Valley, the floor of which was a thousand feet below us, the escarpment on the other side 30 miles away. Whenever I watch the scene in the film *Out of Africa* when Denys Finch Hatton flies Karen Blixen for the first time, the screen opens up and there is the vast expanse of Africa unchanged for millennia, I am reminded of that first view of the Great Gregory Rift. The soundtrack music of Mozart's clarinet concerto in A major conjures it up for me every time.

Social life for European expatriates in Nairobi revolved largely around three clubs. The Nairobi club had been established right at the start of the twentieth century, a few years after Nairobi was born as a depot for the construction of the Uganda Railway. It was a very traditional colonial club with imposing buildings and membership by invitation only, and was frequented largely by embassy people and the few remaining white civil servants. In stark contrast the Muthaiga Club, a decade or so younger and from the start the Nairobi home of the White Highlands set, had a raffish air, described thus by Beryl Markham in her evocative 1942 memoir *West with the Night*: 'Its broad lounge, its bar, its dining-room — none so elaborately furnished as to make a rough-handed hunter pause at its door, nor yet so dowdy as to make a diamond pendant swing ill at ease — were rooms in which the people who made the Africa I knew danced and talked and laughed, hour after hour.'

Membership of the Muthaiga Club was also by invitation and potential members were vetted by the committee; when I was proposed for membership a few years after we arrived, one of the committee, with whom I shared an alma mater, said, 'It'll be good to have another Old Harrovian in the club; there are six Etonians on the committee and only three Harrovians.' That three-quarters of the committee of a social club in an independent African country were drawn from two English public schools says much about the pervasiveness of the British colonial heritage. The third club, Parkland's, was much younger and open to all comers and, while it didn't have the imposing buildings of the Nairobi Club or the bullet-scarred mahogany of the Muthaiga, it was cheap and cheerful, had an acceptable swimming pool, hockey and cricket pitches and a large bar and restaurant. It was best suited for young expatriates on short-term contracts; we were duly introduced by George and Dolly and became regular visitors.

It was a feature of expatriate life led far from home that friendships were easily made – a circle of friends was essential after leaving our families and support networks far away – and just as easily lost when friends were posted elsewhere. With no email or international phone calls most then disappeared from your life. Being at the tail end of the colonial era we arrived, as one did at the time, armed with a few introductions. A couple were fellow Old Harrovians: Paddy Cliffe, sales director of the local Peugeot dealer and twice winner of the East African Safari Rally, and William O'Brien ('Wob') Lindsay, one time Chief Justice of Sudan. Two others were contacts of my father through his Burnham-on-Crouch friends: Peter Gaymer, wide-boy Essex farmer transplanted to Kenya, wheeling and dealing with local politicians, and Bob Wilson, from the Scottish borders, with a wonderful farm on the Northern slopes of Mount Kenya. These four characters, with very large personalities, were long-term residents of Kenya but people with whom at the time I had little in common.

Within a few weeks, instead, we began to find our own friends through the clubs and through work, and nurtured the friendships with frequent entertaining. We had established our little home and reliable transport and a small circle of friends. We were ready for the adventures of life in Africa.

3. FAMILY LIFE

FOR OUR FIRST SEVEN YEARS in Africa we lived in our little flat, seeing no reason to move. We settled into a comfortable routine; with my commute to the office in central Nairobi at that time being a drive of no more than ten minutes, I was able to come home for the hour and a half lunch break. My office hours were from 8.30 till 4.30 Monday to Friday and 8.30 till 12.30 on Saturdays: it took a while for the ex-colonies to shed the outdated work routines of 1950s Britain. Fairly often my work took me away from home but I knew that Bente and Marina would be well looked after by our neighbours. At that time security in Nairobi was not the problem it has since become.

The spouses of expatriates on work permits were not themselves permitted to take paid employment, so many of them occupied themselves with unpaid voluntary work. Not long after we arrived Bente got such a job, teaching English to the children at the local Cheshire Home, an orphanage housed in the Nairobi Orthopaedic Hospital. When, three months after we arrived, we celebrated Marina's second birthday, we arranged for a minibus to bring half a dozen of these children to our flat where we had a party in the garden. Among them was a mischievous little three year old who had been born with a growth on his tongue causing his lower jaw to be slightly enlarged and crooked. His mother was unable to care for him and he was given into the care of the Cheshire Home. This was William Ireri, who gradually became part of our family, first as a regular visitor, then staying overnight and coming with us for weekend trips, eventually joining us back in the UK where he has lived happily for more than 30 years. He has called me Dad all his adult life.

When Bente was not giving her English classes to the children at the Amani Cheshire Home she would often walk the half-mile to the centre of Westlands to do the household shopping, leaving it with Mr. Singh, the greengrocer, for me to collect on my way home from work.

Mr Singh became almost a family friend. He sat all day and every day behind the till of his busy shop from where we bought fruit which was to us wonderfully exotic, woven baskets of oranges, green but ripe, mangoes in their many varieties, avocados, passion fruit, pawpaw and the limes with which they should always be paired. We found out that he also owned a dairy farm and was a wealthy man; I saw him once checking his bank statement, sneaked a glance and saw a balance in excess of £100,000 in his current account. He was a widower living with his mother and we were once privileged to be invited to his home for dinner. 'Mummy', a little bird of a woman in her eighties, bustled round in her beautiful sari serving us delicious food, after which Mr Singh (I could never bring myself to call him by his given name Joginder and never learnt his true family name) brought out his whisky, to 'Mummy's' obvious disapproval. Years later, on a visit back to Nairobi, I called in to his shop to be told by his son that he was in hospital for an operation. I visited him, knocked on his door, went in and saw him for the first time without his turban and beard net, lying back with a wonderful mane of hair and beard surrounding his strong and lined old face like a huge halo, looking for all the world like an Old Testament prophet.

A few months after we arrived, on my drive to work I began to notice the same young African man walking up to Westlands each morning. One day it was raining. I felt sorry for him and gave him a lift. From then on I regularly stopped for him. He told me his name was Seven and he came from Western Kenya. His hearing appeared to be attuned to the distinctive sound of my VW Beetle's air-cooled engine. Given that perhaps one in five cars was a VW beetle I found it quite uncanny that he would ignore all the others, but as soon as he heard mine he would stop, turn round and give me a slow gentle smile. Our conversations were brief but wide-ranging considering his limited life experience and I enjoyed his company. Then one day he asked me if I could lend him ten shillings towards the cost of returning to his home town for a family funeral which, of course, I did. I never saw him again. I do not know whether there was indeed a funeral and he suffered some accident on the long journey or whether he was simply embarrassed that he had had to ask for money. After that my morning commute was a little less interesting.

On Sunday evenings the restaurant at Parklands was given over to dancing and singing. Like many other young couples we would leave our small children in the car; an askari, a watchman, patrolled the car park and if he heard a child crying he would immediately come in and alert the parents, knowing which child belonged to whom. Towards the end of the evening, with the men in particular well lubricated by excellent Kenyan beer, singing would take over from dancing; one or two people had guitars and we would go through a regular repertoire ranging from American folk to schmaltzy Roger Whittaker ballads, Roger being a local boy made good. The man who often led the singing, Jim Simons, typified the entrepreneurial spirit which ran through Nairobi in those heady post-independence days. Jim had discovered some caves a hundred miles or so outside Nairobi with guano many feet deep, deposited over the centuries by the large resident bat colony. He made a good living selling it to farmers, employing a small gang of workers to dig it out.

Most weekends we would venture out from Nairobi, the choice of places to visit being large and varied. Regular trips were to the soda lakes of Magadi and Nakuru with their huge populations of flamingos, the half-million-year-old site of early human settlement at Olorgesailie, Nairobi Game Park and the animal orphanage at its entrance, and of course Lake Naivasha, a sixty square mile sweet-water lake some fifty miles from Nairobi. William from the Cheshire Home, who became a regular visitor, sometimes joined us on day trips; I recall him struggling gamely up the boggy slopes of Mount Kenya far above the treeline.

The drive to Naivasha took us through the forests north of the city, along the rim of the Rift Valley, with the breathtaking view which never palled into familiarity, and down the escarpment to the floor of the valley, descending 1,000 feet by a series of precipitous hairpin bends. Halfway down there was a small chapel erected in memory of the Italian prisoners of war who built the road, some of whom lost their lives in doing so. The road continued along the floor of the valley through dry grazing land, giraffe and antelope mingling comfortably with the domestic cattle, and through a stand of magnificent old yellow-barked acacia thorn trees down to the lake. In our early years we would usually have lunch at the charming old Lake Hotel; later we were to acquire an interest in a lakeside property. Later still the wonderful old acacias were cut down to make charcoal, apparently on the instructions of Jomo Kenyatta's venal wife Mama Ngina.

During our time in Kenya a few family members and friends made the considerable effort to visit us – intercontinental travel was not as simple then as it has become – and we had the great pleasure of introducing them to the country we had come to love. Our first visitors were my parents-in-law, Lis and Erik, whom I will refer to by the names my daughters gave them, *Mormor* (literally Mothermother, i.e., maternal grandmother) and *Boddy*, Marina's first attempt at *bedstefar*, grandfather, after we had been in Nairobi for a year. Boddy had introduced me to the excellent Danish beer when I first met him eight years earlier; I in turn introduced him to the excellent Kenyan beer, served in bottles twice the size. Like most Danes he loved singing, and we had a couple of very enjoyable Sunday evenings singing and drinking at Parklands club, after which I drove home cautiously along the unmade back roads and he conveniently forgot he was a policeman. While they were staying we made our first visit to the coast, of which I write later. From then on they visited almost every year.

A month after their first visit our second daughter Margaret was born. I had been present at Marina's birth, a very moving experience, but the more old-fashioned Nairobi Hospital frowned on such things so I had to wait outside during the long and difficult delivery. Jeannie became part-time nanny and Margaret spent as much time in her makeshift sling as she did with Bente and me. I recall, not long after she was born, taking a trip to Olorgesailie, wandering among the prehistoric hand-axes and hippo bones with my two-month-old baby daughter sleeping soundly on Jeannie's back. We did not know at the time that Jeannie herself was in the early stages of pregnancy, a baby born prematurely the following Christmas and only surviving a couple of days.

A few months later my own parents came out to visit, the only time they did so in the nine years we lived in Kenya. Soon after their arrival I took them for a late afternoon drive through the Nairobi Game Park in my VW Beetle. There is an area of acacia forest quite close to the main entrance and, as we drove slowly through it on a narrow sandy side track, we turned a corner to see a large old bull buffalo blocking our way. Buffaloes are herd animals, quite placid in a group, but a solitary bull has often been rejected by the herd and can be unpredictable. We stopped and he stared at us balefully: we were invading his space and he wasn't happy. After a few seconds, with no warning whatsoever, he dropped his head and charged, half a ton of solid malevolent beef with quite unexpected acceleration. I had taken the precaution of shifting into reverse gear and I floored the accelerator: I had no idea a Beetle could go backwards quite so fast. After what seemed an age but was only a few seconds, when he was within a couple of metres of our front bumper, with our wheels throwing up gritty sand in his eyes, he obviously decided he had made his point, slowed to a walk and ambled off into the trees. Dad, ever ready with a witty comment, asked if there was a laundry nearby.

Wild animals of course were a constant in life in East Africa. One Saturday we had been out late the evening before, we were going to the theatre and unusually I had an afternoon nap. Bente woke me from a deep sleep to tell me there was a monkey in the kitchen. I got up, slightly disorientated, went to investigate and found a large Sykes monkey which had come in through an open window to plunder a bowl of fruit sitting on the work top with a 'come and get me' expression. I approached nervously as Sykes are big monkeys weighing nearly 10 kgs. It took refuge in a cupboard with sliding double doors; I slid the doors open, it hid down the other end and after a few goes it was obvious that it wasn't going to emerge of its own accord. I must outwit it, I thought, tied some string to a banana and threw it to him thinking he wouldn't let go and I could pull him out. Right on the first part, wrong on the second; he caught it, braced himself against the cupboard frame, peeled and ate the banana then threw the skin back to me. I called a hunter of our acquaintance for advice. Sounding as if he too had been woken early from a nap he suggested I put on gloves and reach in and haul it out, considerably easier said than done – for a start gloves don't come easily to hand in tropical Africa. Eventually I gave a set of golf clubs to a couple of the house boys and we left for the theatre. When we returned the monkey was gone; I didn't ask how they managed it, I probably wouldn't have liked the answer.

In addition to the visits by our parents we had some other family visitors. My aunt Christina Foyle and her husband Ron called in for a couple of days en route to South Africa for her usual tax-deductible winter stay: Foyles maintained a branch in Cape Town and she had a house nearby. They came to our little flat for dinner and I asked how their flight had been.

'Very comfortable,' said Auntie Chrissie. 'We flew first class.' A pause, then, 'I don't know why everyone doesn't fly first class, it's so much nicer.' She led a cushioned life and I think she was genuinely puzzled.

My sister Tina visited twice, once with her first husband Dick and their two children Chrissie and Lawrence, then some years later with Jim, who was eventually to become her second husband. On the first visit we drove down to Kitani Lodge in Tsavo Game Park in a borrowed Peugeot 404. A mile or so before we reached the lodge the track crossed a stream and, used to my rear-engined VW Beetle, I thought we would have less chance of getting stuck if I took the crossing at speed. The result was soaked electrics and a dead engine. I decided to walk to the lodge to get help but, when I armed myself with the jack handle and my brother-in-law suggested that it would not offer much defence against an irate elephant, common sense took over and we simply waited for the engine to dry out in the warm sunshine.

I have very fond memories, refreshed from time to time when I look at old colour slides, of that stay at Kitani. It was a self-catering cottage of two rooms and a covered veranda with a simple outdoor kitchen in front, facing Mount Kilimanjaro, which filled the western horizon. In the evening, after the children had gone to bed, we sat on the veranda, chatting by the light of a hurricane lamp. This of course attracted flying insects including a large goliath beetle, one of the largest insects on earth with a chunky body more than four inches long. It climbed ponderously up the back of Tina's shirt while she was completely absorbed gazing at Kilimanjaro in the moonlight, unaware of its presence until I flicked it off before it could reach the bare flesh of her shoulder. I love the large mammals and reptiles of Africa but have also found great fascination in its rich insect life, watching a dung-beetle trundling the ball of buffalo faeces in which its eggs are kept cosy and warm, or a praying mantis gradually dismembering a daddy longlegs hypnotically drawn to it. Individually insects are fascinating; in a swarm they can be terrifying. My first experience of the enormous impact they can make was the first time we experienced the heavy rains, a signal to termites that it is their time to fly and establish their own nests in the rain-softened soil. I was driving home from Nairobi when they swarmed and my windscreen wipers could not cope, mashing the fleshy insects to an opaque pulp. The next morning our doorstep and outside windowsills were carpeted with the gossamer of shed wings and many thousands of now-flightless termites were crawling around defenceless, a feast for the birds. There are also caterpillars whose mass migrations will bring trains to a halt and, of course, locusts which periodically devastate agriculture in the desert north. The great wildebeest migrations of the Mara and Serengeti are impressive, but insect migrations have more impact.

The previous year we had visited with my parents-in-law and had our sleep interrupted by an elephant nibbling at the *makuti* roof; this time it was a hyena which disturbed our sleep, rummaging for a while in our dustbins. In the morning Bente cooked us all breakfast on the outdoor charcoal grill. The pleasure of sitting on a cool crisp morning eating a full English breakfast while gazing across the plains of Africa at its highest mountain defies my powers of description: certainly it ticked many of my boxes.

When Tina and Jim visited some years later they decided to take themselves off for a few days in our Renault 16, comfortable enough but not really designed as a cross-country vehicle. Trusting the road map we gave them they headed south, intending to reach Lake Magadi. What the map didn't show was that where the railway line crossed the unmade road it was up to the motorists to construct their own crossing. They did so laboriously, building ramps from whatever material they could find.

It is strange but nice that friends who would pass within a couple of miles of us in the UK without bothering to say hello would make detours of hundreds of miles to see us when we lived in Africa. At various times we had visits from a few Foyle cousins, and friends from my earlier life: Tony Jones, a friend since my nursery-school days, now resident in Nepal; Mandy Hutton Squire, a girlfriend from my teen years and now living in South Africa; David Steiber with whom I served my accountancy articles in London, now in Geneva; and Hubert Reid, a school friend who had been best man at our wedding. I am still in contact with all of them.

We were not earning significantly more than we would have done back in Europe – it was not till the explosion of development in the Middle East that expatriate salaries became very inflated. Like most of our friends we were on a tight budget and good restaurants were expensive, so a large part of our social life was home entertaining; we would have dinner with friends a couple of times a week. Good meat, fruit and vegetables were cheap and plentiful and with the great range of climatic conditions most things were in season year round. Bente was an excellent cook (it wasn't till many years later when circumstances dictated it that I discovered my own love of cooking) and if we decided on a whim to entertain we could buy fillet steak, fresh strawberries and cream for a fraction of the cost back home and she would prepare a delicious meal in no time, helped by knowing that Jeannie was there to do the washing up.

I can only recall one time when I did the cooking. Bente and the girls were in Denmark, where I was to join them a couple of weeks later for my first home leave, and I invited some friends for dinner. I decided to cook steak and kidney pudding, a childhood favourite of mine not part of Bente's repertoire, and to save time did so in a pressure cooker. I can only surmise at the cause of the explosion. I assume that as the pudding rose the cloth covering it blocked the pressure-relief valve. The results were dramatic: the safety valve blew out, hitting the ceiling like a bullet, followed by most of the cloth through which was strained the contents of the pudding. My friends arrived to find me in shock and the meal spread around the kitchen. We eventually dined on sandwiches and I never quite removed the gravy stains from the ceiling.

Jeannie made me a light breakfast every morning and provided one other small culinary memory. Usually she gave me toast and marmalade, occasionally grilled tomatoes on toast. One day she tried a variation by combining the two – I persuaded her not to repeat the experiment.

In our small flat, entertaining was usually limited to one other couple but even so the evenings often ended with dancing. Bente and I both liked the same music, that of the 1930s and '40s, Glenn Miller, Benny Goodman, Louis Armstrong and of course the incomparable Ella. Inevitably the wine encouraged us to crank up the volume and often a bleary-eyed little Marina would emerge from her room and join us in dancing, accompanied, as soon as she was old enough to toddle, by Margaret. They developed a love of music and dancing, as in her turn did their younger sister Emma when she came into our lives ten years later. This has been passed on to their own children, most of whom are wonderfully musical. Some years ago, when on holiday in Borneo with Emma and her family, I looked after her two boys James and Oliver, then aged five and three, while their parents trekked up Mount Kinabalu. For the boys it was their first night without their mother; initially they were distraught. I put on some music, Glenn Miller, the three of us danced together and they calmed down. I found it quite poignant that the music to which their aunts had danced in Africa at that same age could calm their nephews fifty years later in the jungles of Borneo.

Marina and Margaret went to playgroups, then nursery schools and eventually to The Banda, a private primary school in Langata, a suburb out towards the Ngong Hills. I would drop them at the bus stop in Westlands on my way to work and they would be collected by a battered old minibus, which brought them back in the late afternoon. The five-acre site through which the single-storey school buildings rambled was on the edge of forest land, with monkeys, giraffes and antelope regular visitors. Academic standards were high and we felt that they were getting a good start to their education. The school was racially mixed and I recall walking with Marina behind two of her classmates, one European, one African. Marina said, 'That's my friend Susan.'

'Which one?' I asked.

'The one in the red dress,' she replied.

When we eventually returned to the UK the choice of school was to dictate where we lived. To go from such idyllic surroundings to a modern glass and concrete urban setting would have been a significant culture shock on top of the stress of relocation from the warm sunshine of Africa to the UK's northern European climate. Fortunately we found a school occupying three large converted Edwardian houses set in the woodlands of Hindhead, in Surrey; it lacked the giraffes, of course, but they both slotted in comfortably.

Jeannie was an intelligent young woman and eventually we arranged for her to attend secretarial classes. I had by then left Gill and Johnson and begun working with Jeff Fulmer, of whom I'll write later, and Jeannie joined the company doing clerical work. She was replaced as our house girl by her best friend Mary Muthoni, who was to remain with us for the rest of our time in Kenya and eventually live with us for a couple of years in the UK. Mary's father had not been as enlightened as Jeannie's father Njoroge, and did not believe in education for girls. She told us that if he ever found her with a book he would throw it on the fire. Coming from a family of strong women I have always found such attitudes not only despicable but incomprehensible; why attempt to deny us the fruits of the intelligence of half the population? Extraordinary, and extraordinarily stupid.

After seven years in our little flat we moved to a house, a three-bedroomed bungalow built from the traditional butchered stone blocks, the lower courses stained red with rain-splashes from the murram soil. It sat on a one-acre plot in Peponi Road, a few hundred yards upstream on the same small river as the flat. The garden was not as attractive, mostly rough grass and some unkempt flower beds with a few trees shading us from the road, but the house was considerably larger. There were servants' quarters where Mary and the gardener John lived. Mary told us she had a house of her own near her home town of Nakuru where she also had a house girl, paid from her own very modest salary: thus is wealth distributed in Africa.

There were other less benign ways in which wealth was redistributed. With the enormous differential between the rich and the poor, burglary and petty theft were understandably common. One of the favoured methods of burglary was pole fishing, where the burglar attaches a hook to a long pole, pokes it through an open window and uses it to surreptitiously remove bedding and clothing. To deter the victim from grabbing the pole should they wake, it was usually embedded with razor blades and protruding nails. We fell victim to this type of burglary only once, while we were still living in the flat. I always woke before Bente and on Sundays I sometimes drove Jeannie to church before breakfast. On one such time I returned home to be met by Bente with: 'Where are they?'

'Where are what?'

'The curtains, of course!'

I am not the most observant of people and had not noticed, when I got up and walked through the living room, that we had left a window open and an enterprising burglar had unhooked the full-length curtains and neatly extracted them through the security grille.

In Peponi Road we had a night-watchman, Stephen, provided by an agency, who was with us throughout the two years we lived there. He would arrive each evening punctually at six and stay till six the next morning, seven days a week, with a couple of weeks' annual leave when he would return to his own family in Western Kenya. He was a delightful and reassuring presence, would play with Marina and Margaret, prowl the garden at night to deter burglars and always be there to open the gate with a welcoming smile no matter what time we returned from our frequent evenings out.

In the large L-shaped living room we equipped the dining area with a locally made table, chairs and sideboard and engaged a carpenter to make for us a couple of sofas, low tables and shelving units for books and hi-fi, all from Elgon olive, a beautiful pale-coloured local hardwood. I had never before made anything of any significance but decided I would make our own bed. I went to the major timberyard and asked for some wood; they asked what kind; I asked what they had. They trotted out a long list of tree species, most of which I had never heard of but including mahogany, which sounded familiar, so I chose that. Back home I discovered that mahogany is almost as hard as concrete but I persevered and eventually we had a large and exceptionally sturdy bed. When we finally came to leave Kenya we decided to leave our furniture behind, thinking we could easily replace it with the equivalent quality made in the UK, a decision which I much regret.

Having designed the built-in shelving for the house so that hi-fi units would fit exactly we had a break-in and of course the only thing taken was the hi-fi. When I replaced it the retailer was a little surprised that the most important criterion was not the sound quality but the external dimensions.

I look back on our family life in Africa as a time of great happiness. I was living in a beautiful country which exceeded all my childhood expectations of Africa, and my professional life was varied and interesting. Because I was away from my own country, with its familiar influences of extended family and childhood friends, my own little nuclear family became the major focus of my life, to be cherished and enjoyed. Bente was fulfilled in her work at the Cheshire home and our two little daughters were healthy and beginning to show the interest in life and in things around them that they have retained to this day; I was content with life and excited by its prospects.

4. THE ROMANCE OF AUDIT

MANY YEARS AFTER LEAVING AFRICA I was in Moscow discussing with a major Russian accountancy firm the preparation of a joint bid to modernise the antiquated Russian state audit systems. I asked the partner in charge how we could divide the work. He replied, 'We will provide the technical detail, we would like you to add the romance, the poetry.' I thought at the time that only a Russian could see poetry and romance in audit, but looking back on my career I decided that whenever I wrote my autobiography there would be a chapter entitled 'The Romance of Audit'. Here it is.

On my first day in the Nairobi office, after Ted Johnson introduced me to the staff, he surprised me by telling me that, in addition to the routine work of an audit senior, I was to establish and manage a new department, Systems and Investigations. I soon found out that the firm had not moved with the times and, as they intended to strengthen the relationship with Deloitte International, they had to introduce modern auditing techniques. The experience I had gained at Price Waterhouse in Copenhagen apparently equipped me to do this. I was not of course to get paid any more or to have any dedicated staff in my embryonic department, but it did mean that my work was more interesting and varied.

I was also told on day one that I was to spend one week each month supervising two small offices in Northern Tanzania, in the towns of Arusha and Moshi, some 50 miles apart. On my first trip there, a month or so after I arrived, I found out why: the local partner, a Scot, was a temperamental alcoholic no longer on speaking terms with the Nairobi partners, and I had to mediate between them. Mediation was not easy as Mr. McNeill took to his bed on hearing of my impending visit and did not resurface until I left. Not once in the couple of years I was visiting the offices did I meet him. It was not ideal, but the wonderful five-hour drive on dirt roads, dodging giraffe and zebra, being for the first time in complete charge of a small office, having a beer with the few other professional staff at the end of the day, the only European in the bar, and the general joyful unpredictability of Africa made it worthwhile.

The first time I drove down to Arusha I was immediately in the Africa of which I had dreamt since childhood, the Africa of Hemingway and Rider Haggard, of G. A. Henty and Wilfred Robinson. I left our little flat in Westlands well before first light, to get on the road before the heavy lorries which would be throwing up their clouds of dust. Twenty miles south-east down the Mombasa road I turned off, just after the little town of Athi River, later to become a significant part of our social life. Ahead lay the main road to Tanzania, 150 miles of sand and gravel. It weaved its way between rolling green hills, studded with groves of acacia thorn trees and home to uncountable numbers of animals, thousands upon thousands of zebra and wildebeest, stately families of giraffe, herds of buffalo, joyful groups of impala and gazelle: my heart sang. I recall taking a sandy bend slightly too fast and losing control of my little VW Beetle, making an uncontrolled slide under the outstretched neck of a giraffe, who simply looked down on me with that elegant disdain that giraffes do so well.

The border with Tanzania was at the little town of Namanga where there was a small hotel eking a living from the occasional tourist (this was before the days of mass tourism in East Africa) and offering refreshment to the handful of people like me travelling between the two countries. The first time I stopped there, I was greeted by an elegant Maasai in full traditional costume, idly flicking his spear into a nearby thorn tree.

'I wonder, sir, if I could interest you in buying a spear?' he asked in perfect English.

In conversation I found out that he had been educated in the UK but, after considering all options, decided that the traditional Maasai way of life appealed more, although he still had some cash requirements which he met by selling spears to tourists.

Another time I was having a quiet coffee there when two middle-aged American ladies arrived and aggressively ordered refreshment: 'We want two cold beers. That's one, two, two cold beers.' I guessed they were not totally enjoying their safari.

I stayed in Arusha at the New Safari Hotel where, on checking in, the receptionist asked if I'd like early morning tea at 6.30. I said seven o'clock would be better. She said it was only available at 6.30. Tourism had not yet had a significant impact.

The staff in the two offices were of course friendly and easy to work with, a handful of unqualified young Asian accountants with African support staff. As an aside it was immediately obvious that, during the colonial period which had only finished a few years earlier, no attempt had been made to bring Africans into the professions; this was very different to the old French and Portuguese colonial legacy where the brightest were taken back to the 'motherland' and given the same education as their colonial masters. I used to go a beer after work with a couple of young Asian men from the Moshi office, and I recall being in an upstairs bar looking out at the snows of Kilimanjaro, much more extensive fifty years ago than they are now, and taking a photo with my old Kodak Retinette camera which I would never have attempted sober. I was, for the first time in my life, the only white person in the room, feeling completely at ease in the company of the young men and women of Africa. I treasure that photo today, a solitary star above the towering crater and the snows which Hemingway made famous shimmering in the moonlight.

One of the first assignments for my embryonic Systems and Investigations Department was a fraud investigation at the East African Portland Cement Company at Athi River. One of the shareholders in the company was the Danish engineering firm F L Schmidth, which had supplied the kiln in which the cement was made. They provided technical expertise by seconding engineers from Denmark and the current secondee, Hans-Eric Borgholm, suspected fraud by the locally employed management. G & J, as auditors, were called in to investigate. The investigation was fairly inconclusive, other than discovering that the general manager had had a 35foot yacht built in the company's workshops with the company's labour and almost certainly all the materials bought by the company. I have sailed since childhood and recognised the names of a well-known yacht chandler cropping up among the purchases, unlikely suppliers for a cement company on the African plains a long way from any open water. However, as good managers were hard to find it was dealt with by a reprimand and, to the best of my knowledge, he got to keep the boat.

For me the best outcome of the assignment was the close friendship we formed with Hans-Eric and his wife Irma, with whom we would have dinner at least once a week, spend long weekends in Tsavo and stay a few times at his company's guest house at Kikambala.

Several of my audits involved trips up country. Kenya's economy was primarily agricultural, and G & J's practice had grown along with the growth of Kenya's agriculture. Our clients included many of the large estates which had been established by European settlers early in the twentieth century, some of which are now private game reserves catering for the top end of the tourist market. From the few days I spent on a tea plantation in the beautiful area around Kericho, I could well understand why those settlers chose Kenya for their home. With their covering of densely planted tea bushes, the tops of which were billiard-table-smooth from being plucked daily, the rolling green hills could, with a little imagination, be the South Downs of Sussex. Add to that the woodland streams teeming with trout and it becomes home from home, with the added advantages of an equable climate, reliable sunshine and plentiful servants.

One of my upcountry audits was Kakuzi Fibrelands, a large sisal plantation which was diversifying into other crops including coffee and green beans, clearing unused bush land to do so. The area was infested with tsetse fly, which require fairly dense bushes to breed and survive. The most cost-effective way of driving out the flies was to use a herd of goats to eat the bushes. Carrying out a stock count of 400 goats in a large, corrugated iron barn, baking in the African sun, is among the more unusual things I have done in the course of my auditing life; certainly it was the smelliest.

Sisal as an economically viable crop was in decline, but I found the whole process of turning large spiky leaves into rope and sacks fascinating. My daughters all have very enquiring minds and I spent a delightful Saturday afternoon with three-year-old Marina, showing her the very direct link between agriculture and everyday objects. I took her to Kakuzi where we watched men cutting the large sisal leaves from the plant then followed the leaves to the rudimentary factory where they were threshed to release the fibres. We saw the fibres, a metre long and brilliant white in the sunshine, lovelier in every way than the oil-based and factory-produced synthetics which have largely replaced them, drying in the sunshine, and watched them getting packed into bales and being shipped out. We followed them to another client a few miles away, East African Bag and Cordage, where we saw those same fibres being spun into rope and twine, and the twine then woven into the fabric from which sacks, largely used in agriculture, were made. This was more than fifty years ago and Marina has long forgotten the experience, but I can still close my eyes and smell the mustiness of the bags and hear the staccato rattle of the shuttles being batted back and forth on the looms.

I also have vibrant visual memories of another crop as beautiful as it is utilitarian, cotton. One of the clients allocated to me was the Kenya Cotton Board. Most of the work was routine, carried out in the Board's small Nairobi offices, but I also visited one of the rural buying operations and the sight of the cotton, raw from the fields, lying in great fluffy white piles waiting to be weighed comes so easily to mind. To digress a little, I learnt at the start of my auditing career that the greater your understanding of what the client actually does, the more effective your audit work will be. I always made a point, at the start of each assignment, of spending some time on the factory floor or the equivalent. To better understand the production of cotton I visited a couple of ginneries, one in Meru district north-east of Mount Kenya, the other at Nambale in a remote part of Western Province close to the border with Uganda. Management of such ginneries was in the hands of Asians, descendants of indentured labourers brought in to build the railway seventy years earlier. Apart from the fairly routine checking of the existence of assets and going through the rudimentary accounting records, these two visits offered me two very different culinary experiences. At the first I discovered the simple pleasure of sitting on the floor round a communal cooking pot with three others sharing a wonderfully spiced mess of lentils scooped out by hand or with pieces of chapati. At the other I arrived accompanied by my wife and two daughters, the younger only a few weeks old, to find that the manager had kindly equipped the guest house with what he considered the essentials for a small European family for three days: a loaf of bread, six eggs, a bottle of gin and a bottle of whisky. Fortunately, he supplemented this with wonderful curries prepared by his wife.

In between the larger assignments I did some smaller and more mundane audits which brought me into contact with some interesting characters. I recall Anders Holmberg, a Swedish hunter who ran eye-wateringly expensive safaris for wealthy individuals, spending months at a time in the bush in large heavy-duty canvas tents, a throwback to earlier times. The tents were made locally by Low & Bonar, another audit client; the quality was such that the Kleberg family regularly sent a plane from the US to pick up similar tents to use on the million-plus acres of their King Ranch in Texas.

Other characters included Don and Maureen Bridge, who set up a small publishing company specialising in tourist guide books to the Arabian Gulf states – they were ten years ahead of their time but sadly the business did not last long enough to benefit from the extraordinary growth seen in the Gulf from the 1970s onwards, and Michaela Denis.

Michaela and her husband Armand had presented the first television wildlife programmes which I remembered and were, of course, heroes of mine. Michaela was a glamorous but fading blonde, Armand bedridden with Parkinson's. I used to go round to their house in Karen on Saturday mornings to sort out their accounts. The second time I went, Michaela greeted me warmly, sashaying down their large staircase, bra-less in a see-through blouse, presumably intent on seduction. I was a fairly shy twenty-six year old, she was double my age and, although my memory clouds over what followed, I believe I clasped my accountant's briefcase protectively in front of me and hurried into the study. Ah, the missed opportunities of life! Some years later, after Armand died, she married Wob Lindsay, by then in his late sixties and to whom I had an 'introduction'. He died shortly after they returned from honeymoon but, according to gossip, with a smile on his lips. Michaela devoted the rest of her very eventful life doing her best to preserve forests through her charity Men of the Trees.

One of my audits introduced me to the hospitality industry

which was later to play a significant part in my up-and-down career. At the turn of the twentieth century an ambitious young man, Abraham Lazarus Block, trekked from South Africa with all his worldly goods on the back of a donkey to seek his fortune in what was then British East Africa. A newly built railway was carrying passengers from the coast to Nairobi in less than a day, a journey which until then had taken weeks, and the country was destined for growth. By dint of hard work Block duly made his fortune, building a chain of hotels which by the time of my arrival was run by his sons, Jack and Tubby.

Block Hotels owned, among others, the New Stanley and the Norfolk Hotels in Nairobi. In the optimism accompanying Kenya's independence major new developments were planned, and Tubby was involved in a project to build a hotel close to the New Stanley in partnership with El Al Israeli Airlines, TWA and Solel Boneh, a major Israeli building contractor. None of the shareholders were actively involved in the day-to-day management of the project, which by default was taken up by the company's solicitor Michael Somen.

Gill and Johnson was appointed to do the audit, a task which fell to me, and Mike, getting little support from the shareholders, took to using me as a sounding board. Money was of course always tight and he had his job cut out raising the necessary finance. The hotel was designed as a twenty-two storey circular tower of bedrooms rising from a podium base housing the reception, restaurants and offices; it was vaguely phallic in design and became known locally as Tubby's erection. One day I was sitting with Mike discussing the cash situation which by then had become quite dire. Construction had been progressing rapidly, the full twenty-two storeys had been built but we didn't have the cash to pay the latest contractor's bill. I suggested to Mike that we might have to remove the top couple of storeys. 'Great idea' he said, 'We'll circumcise the thing!'

Three hundred baths had been ordered for the planned 300 bedrooms, but when they arrived they turned out to be too large for the bathrooms. Fortunately only a couple of floors had reached the fitting-out stage, the rest were redesigned and what was to be a 300-room hotel finished up with 287.

When the hotel eventually opened as the Nairobi Hilton, apart from the usual teething problems found in any large new building everything ran smoothly until the first long rains – East Africa has its 'long rains' in February and March and 'short rains' in October. The main restaurant was on the second floor of the flat-roofed podium from which the tower of bedrooms rose, and a leak appeared in its ceiling. A *fundi*, that useful Swahili word which implies specialist knowledge and skills, was sent into the roof space to fix it. He found that a horizontal drainage pipe carrying the rainwater run-off was leaking and he duly fixed the problem. For almost a year all was fine but with the next long rains the leak reappeared. Another fundi, fortunately endowed with more common sense, went to investigate. He found, suspended from a bracket welded to a steel beam, a bucket which had managed to catch the drips from the short rains but was filled to overflowing by the long. Apparently the welding was excellent and to the best of my knowledge the bucket hangs there to this day.

In January 1970 the King and Queen of Denmark visited Nairobi. As the Ambassador's house didn't have enough rooms to accommodate them they stayed at the Hilton, where a special bed was built to contain the King's nearly-two-metre frame. Shortly after moving to Nairobi we had joined the Danish Society in East Africa and, as I was by then its treasurer, we were invited to the social functions planned for the royal visit.

The Danish Ambassador was new to the country and since his arrival had experienced only unbroken sunshine. His house, by embassy standards, was small but in common with most suburban houses in Nairobi had a large and beautiful garden. His advisors had told him that the pattern of rainfall was completely reliable, the long rains weren't due for another month and he ignored the old hands who warned that, very occasionally, it wasn't – very occasionally the rains came early. The Ambassador went ahead with the large garden party to which some two hundred people were invited. The party was going well, the King and Queen were mingling, the beer was flowing and the sun was shining, until suddenly it wasn't and the heavens opened. Danes, for all their good manners and generally laidback approach to life, can be as determined as anyone when seeking shelter from a tropical downpour and, ignoring the Ambassador's pleas, all two hundred of us rushed for the house where the delightfully relaxed party continued, the Queen half crushed at one end of the large reception room, the King towering over everyone at the other. With the informality which I admire in the Danes there wasn't a security man to be seen and the King and Queen seemed quite unfazed by it all.

The following evening there was a reception held for them in the recently opened Hilton and at some point it was noticed that the King, a difficult person to miss, had gone missing. I was sent to find him and eventually did so; bored by the party in his honour upstairs he had found his way down to the coffee shop on the ground floor where he was enjoying a beer on his own. I sat with him while he finished his beer, then I paid for it (like other monarchs he didn't usually carry cash) and escorted him back to the party upstairs: that was the only time I have bought a King a drink.

One of my more enjoyable small audits was that of Gilbey's Gin, an offshoot of the British company, at the time still a family business. The Nairobi subsidiary was run by Ralph Gilbey, perhaps not a black sheep but certainly someone with whom the rest of the family were more comfortable when he was several thousand miles from head office. At 11 o'clock every morning, instead of arranging a coffee for me he would invite me to his office for a large dry martini. We would discuss many things, some of them alcohol-related so I could justify to myself the additional time spent on the audit, for which of course Gilbey's were happy to pay. I told him once that I occasionally mixed up martinis at home: he asked me how, presumably, like James Bond, enjoying the subtle differences between shaking and stirring. He looked at me in horror when I said that I blended them with ice in a liquidiser.

'But you'll bruise it' was his plaintive response.

The furthest afield I travelled for an audit was Madagascar, the capital city of which is Antananarivo, a name which rolls deliciously off the tongue, though the French, Madagascar's old colonial masters, had rendered it as the slightly less pretty Tananarive, or simply Tana. Being auditors to the Nairobi Hilton we were asked to audit its sister hotel the Madagascar Hilton, under construction near the centre of the city. The first time I went I was on my own and loved it.

I spent hours after work wandering the streets of the old city, a mixture of old Malagasy and more recent French colonial architecture. As with most places which had once been part of the French empire there were restaurants serving excellent French food – I had my first experience of frogs' legs – and edible snails were imported from France. I discovered that although the country had been independent for almost a decade the French had retained a stranglehold on most supplies: I was surprised to find Scottish smoked salmon which had been repacked in France. Every Friday Tana was taken over by an open-air market, supposedly the largest in the world. The vendors, all of whom have, draped round their necks, the large white cotton shawl which will eventually become their winding sheet, begin drifting in from the countryside from early Thursday evening, pushing carts laden with produce and handicrafts and setting up their stalls, which straggle through the whole of the centre of the town. From dawn till dusk it is a gently moving mass of people leisurely browsing and occasionally buying.

I bought a wooden plaque, a bas-relief of animals carved from ebony, hard as stone, and a few of the semi-precious stones which abound in the country: some small amethysts and a yellow citrine. I practised my haggling skills to see how extreme I dared to make my opening offer, eventually getting down to about 25% of the asking price and settling for something over 50%. I recall one protracted negotiation which drew a small crowd and, when the vendor and I finally agreed a price with which we were both happy, there were smiles all round and a modest smattering of applause – Madagascar is a country of warm and friendly people.

With typical disdain for, or ignorance of, local culture the Hilton was built on an old Malagasy burial site and designed as the only high-rise building in Tananarive. The Malagasy people have all the superstitions of their Pacific Ocean relatives and the developers found it hard to recruit labour for the construction. By the time I got there the frame had been completed and fitting out was progressing slowly, having reached the sixth floor, at which point a ghost made its appearance, apparently kicking a labourer in the backside. All work stopped for a few weeks but eventually the less superstitious workers were enticed back and work recommenced. When I returned a year later the hotel was still not complete. There had been more reports of ghosts, but only on the sixth floor, which I chose to avoid.

I was in Tananarive for two weeks on my first visit and at the weekend visited the old castle of Queen Ranavalona I, climbing its many steps followed by gaggle of giggling children – foreign visitors, particularly tall blond Northern Europeans, being rare at the time. I turned suddenly and without any attempt to aim or compose took a photograph which remains one of my favourites: three small children, one of obvious East Asian ancestry, one Indian-looking, the third African. I had learnt that these are the three main strands in the Malagasy population and the altitude at which they each live on that mountainous island are an indication of the order in which each arrived. The first arrivals, the great seafarers from the Far East, had reached the highlands; they were followed by migrants from India who inhabited the lower slopes; last to arrive were Africans from the mainland a few hundred miles to the west, most of whom remained on the coastal plains. Ranavalona's granddaughter, also Ranavalona, figures in one of the wonderful Flashman books by George MacDonald Fraser, from which I learnt more nineteenth-century history than I ever did at school.

I returned to Madagascar the following year, this time with an assistant, Peter Philips, a couple of years younger than me and excellent company. When we completed the audit I decided we had earned a little treat for the journey home. While there were direct daily flights from Tananarive to Nairobi taking a little over three hours, we opted to take the scenic route via the Comoro Islands and Zanzibar. The world's fourth largest island, Madagascar is surprisingly long, a thousand miles from north to south. The distance between towns over the mountainous terrain is too great to cover easily by bus so the old DC-3 Dakotas operated on internal routes by Air Madagascar acted as the local buses, taking ordinary people to visit friends or to take their produce to market. We covered the 400 miles to the northern tip of the island in three hops and it was the first, and probably the last, time I have seen someone get on an aeroplane with chickens in a crate and a winding sheet round their necks.

The last stop before leaving Madagascar was the beautiful Nosy Bé, a cliché of a tropical island, with its gently waving palm trees and white sand beaches. We stretched our legs at the small airfield by the beach and transferred to a more modern plane, a thirty-seater twin-engined turboprop of Air Comore which carried us west via Mayotte and Anjouan to Grand Comore, where we had a four-hour stopover.

A taxi took us into the capital Moroni, a couple of miles from the airport, where we found the only hotel and stepped back in time. The islands, still a colony of France, were home to a large number of expatriate French and families had come straight from Church for their weekly Sunday lunch. The décor was Edwardian brown, fans revolved slowly, creakily and ineffectively in the ceiling, the men wore suits with shirts and ties, and the restaurant was almost full. Foreign visitors were rare and as we entered a silence, almost hostile, fell, the French disdain for the English no less apparent in the colonies than it was in rural France. We took one of the last empty tables by the window, looking out over a beach of black volcanic sand. The hum of conversation slowly picked up and we enjoyed an excellent meal, a salad of hearts of palm followed by a near-perfect steak, the high standards of French cuisine extending to their overseas possessions.

After lunch we relaxed on the beach until it was time to return to the airport for our onward flight but, being a Sunday afternoon, taxis were few and far between and unwilling to stop for a couple of Englishmen. Eventually we found a small Renault which had run out of petrol and, in our halting French, persuaded the driver to take us to the airport in exchange for pushing him to a petrol station couple of hundred yards away. We finally reached the airport just in time to catch the flight. The small plane was full and the steward, apparently not fully recovered from his Saturday night, unlocked the drinks cupboard for us and settled down to sleep, not waking till we landed in Zanzibar.

The final leg of the journey, in an East African Airways DC-9 to Nairobi, was far and away the least interesting. We had left Tana early in the morning and got home late at night. The direct flight would have brought us home in a few hours but would not have been nearly as much fun.

A few months later Peter moved on, taking a job in the Cayman Islands, which was just beginning to develop as an offshore finance centre under the enlightened governor Tom Russell. I got to know Tom as a friend twenty-five years later when he and I were the London representatives of the Cayman Islands and the Turks and Caicos respectively. Peter and I corresponded for a while. I remember him telling me that on the small island of Cayman Brac there were only two roads and only two cars using them: late one New Year's Eve they collided.

Eventually we lost touch; when I visited Grand Cayman twenty years later he had moved on.

Many years later, on the island of Grand Turk, I was listening to the commentary on one of the US networks, of the opening ceremony of the 1992 Olympic Games. The commentator, proud to display his ignorance, said, 'Now here comes the delegation from Madagascar', drawing out the first and third syllables. 'Who the hell knows where Madagascar is?'

Warm memories came flooding back and I smiled and thought, I do.

In my late teens, with my interest in all things African, I watched Bernhard Grzimek's wonderful film *Serengeti Shall Not Die*; ten years later, having come to love the wildlife of East Africa, I did the audit of the Serengeti Research Institute which had been set up in 1966. My wife drove me at dawn to Wilson Airport, Nairobi's original airport which, since its replacement was built a few miles away at Embakasi has been exclusively for light aircraft. There I met with John King, a Nairobi-based vet attached to the Institute who was to fly me down.

It was utterly magical to take off from Wilson for my first-ever flight in a light plane, a small high-winged Cessna 180, to clear the perimeter fence and climb over the Nairobi Game Park, passing on our left the Ngong Hills, and head south-west a couple of thousand feet above the endless plains of East Africa under a cloudless early-morning sky. John had a map strapped to his knee and navigated visually by the occasional small mountain and lake, there being no significant roads or settlements in the 150 miles we covered.

After an hour he pointed and said, 'The strip is just to the right of that kopje.' To me the little rocky hill straight ahead looked identical to a hundred others we had passed but he knew the terrain. He throttled back, lowered the flaps and brought the little plane down in a bumpy landing on a stony strip almost indistinguishable from the surrounding plains. After a few minutes an old Land Rover arrived to drive us the few hundred yards to the Institute. On the way we passed an extraordinary tableau: a wildebeest lay on its side, obviously sedated, and a young man knelt beside it sucking at its haunch.

'That's Peter, our tick man. The only way to harvest the ticks undamaged is to suck them out.'

Amazing what people will do in the interests of research.

The settlement itself was a circle of a dozen or so bungalows with the laboratories and office off to one side. There were a number of scientists, mostly European, some single, some married couples, living in the neat little houses. They were there to study the rich diversity of the 12,000 square miles of the Serengeti ecosystem, home to one of the greatest congregations of wildlife in the world, from elephants roaming in their large and sociable families to ticks on a wildebeest's bottom. I had a room in the guest house and the use of an ancient Land Rover, the steering mechanism of which was fairly idiosyncratic, as I was to find out. Although the distances were all walkable I was reminded that there were dangerous animals about which I should treat with respect.

The audit itself was routine; everything else about the three-day visit was not. The first evening I was invited to dinner by a Dutch couple in a bungalow the other side of the small settlement, together with half a dozen others. I wore, of course, a suit and a tie, this being a time when professional people dressed formally when on business no matter where. The other men wore dinner jackets, their wives long dresses – standards were maintained even in the bush ten miles from the nearest other humans. We had an excellent dinner in enjoyable and relaxed company. I was tired from my pre-dawn start, so when the brandy and cigars appeared I excused myself and went out to the old Land Rover.

I started the engine, turned on the lights and sat

mesmerized as thirteen lions walked between my car and the steps of the bungalow, quite oblivious to my presence. I was told later that they were often around, they were treated with respect by the humans who they in turn ignored. It was a dramatic reminder that the Serengeti belonged to the animals. We were there on sufferance.

The following evening I drove with John to Seronera Lodge ten miles away for dinner. He was excellent company, having spent much of his life in Kenya, and we stayed late, chatting and enjoying a few drinks by the log fire before setting off back to the Institute. John was relaxed and immediately fell asleep so I drove cautiously – fortunately there was only one road and we were, of course, the only vehicle on it. However, in East Africa people are not the only road users: I rounded a bend and my headlights picked up a small group of elephants blocking the way.

I woke John. 'What do I do?'

He muttered drowsily, 'Drive round them, of course,' and promptly went back to sleep.

I turned gingerly off the road and bumped through the bush, the vehicle's dodgy steering fighting me every yard, and rejoined the road 100 yards beyond the elephants, which never even acknowledged our presence.

I finished my work at lunchtime the following day and, having a few hours before we were due to fly back to Nairobi, I persuaded one of the African guides to take me for a drive. In the space of a few miles we saw large numbers of the plains game for which the Serengeti is famous: buffalo, wildebeest, giraffe, zebra and the many species of antelope, little families of warthogs trotting along with their antenna-tails erect, and a few elephants. Finally, to round off what had been a fascinating trip, a mile or so before we got back to the settlement the guide stopped the car and pointed to the left. Stretched out in the shade of a bush a few yards from the road was a leopard, the only one of the big five I had, till then, failed to find in the two years I had been visiting Kenya's rich game parks. We sat and watched him for a while before returning to the guest house where John picked me up and flew us back to Nairobi.

Auditing is usually thought to be boring; I have always enjoyed it for its variety. During my ten years as an auditor I dipped oil tanks at a refinery in Northern Jutland at midnight on a New Year's Eve, counted carnations in Twickenham, biscuits in Aarhus and goats at Kakuzi, and avoided a ghost in the Madagascar Hilton, but as auditing memories go nothing will match those few days in Serengeti. Sadly a few years later relations between Kenya and Tanzania deteriorated and the Institute was disbanded, its valuable research discontinued.

The game of the Serengeti is magnificent but sometimes it is the smaller life forms which can add drama to life. One of the G & J partners, John Highwood, lived in a beautiful house near Limuru, a dozen or so miles north of Nairobi where the hills rise towards the Aberdare mountains. It was a typical large stone bungalow sitting on the side of a valley, its beautiful gardens running down to a small dam; on the opposite slope was 50 acres of tea plantation, the income from which nicely supplemented John's earnings from the partnership. I suspect his background was not quite as genteel as he wanted us to believe, but every year he and his wife Audrey lived up to the image which they tried to project and gave a tea party for the staff. Thirty or so of us would stand around in the garden sipping tea from delicate china cups and eating elegant little cucumber sandwiches.

One year a colony of army ants chose that day to go hunting through the garden. When army ants migrate from one nest to another they do so in a single file, with the large soldiers patrolling no more than a few inches from the main trail, which is very visible and to be avoided. When they hunt they fan out in a wide arc, invisible beneath the matted grass. If they find a warm body they climb, unseen and unfelt, to investigate. They are sensitive to any movements and if they feel threatened will sink their extremely sharp pincers into the soft flesh of their target. They appear able to communicate with each other and when one bites, they all bite. The sight of thirty apparently genteel people ripping off underwear to remove their attackers, the ladies trying to retain some vestige of dignity by hiding behind bushes, the men shamelessly dropping their trousers where they stood, was hilarious, straight out of the *Carry On* playbook.

A couple of times the Highwoods asked us to house-sit when they went on extended leave to the UK and of course we jumped at the opportunity. Much as we liked our little flat it was wonderful to spend a few weeks in a large house in such a beautiful setting, with a log fire every evening – at an altitude of more than two thousand metres the evenings could be quite chilly. The houseboy shared the genteel pretensions of his employers and would not speak Swahili, in his view the language of servants. Swahili is a rich language with Bantu roots, most of the words ending in a vowel. As over the centuries the Bantu culture was influenced by contact with Europeans new words were created, usually by adding a vowel to the borrowed word. Toast became *tosti*, soap, *sapon* in French, became *sabuni*, a small farm, *champs* in French became *shamba*. To demonstrate his superiority over other servants he pointedly avoided such Swahili words: one day he announced that he would be serving us tea on the 'troll'.

As my initial contract with Gill and Johnson came to an end in 1969, I was offered a partnership in the company, which by then had become a fully-fledged member of the Deloitte group. I would have been, at the age of twenty-eight, one of the youngest partners in Deloitte's worldwide. It was of course very tempting but at that time to become a partner in a professional practice was very much a long-term commitment. Partnerships were not bought and sold with the fluidity of the giant professional practices of today, and in the UK professional partnerships were still limited to twenty members. Instead I signed a new two-year contract and took my six weeks of home leave, divided between

Denmark and the UK, staying with family.

I returned to Nairobi a couple of weeks before my wife and daughters. As there was nothing of any great interest on local television, which was limited to a single government-controlled black and white channel, I had plenty of time to indulge my love of reading. A few of the books I have read in my life left such an impression that I can remember when and where I read them: Rider Haggard's *King Solomon's Mines* in the sick bay at my prep school when I was twelve; Hemingway's *The Old Man and the Sea* one quiet Sunday in our cosy flat in Copenhagen when I was twenty-four; and Tolkien's wonderful Lord of the Rings when I was getting back into life in Kenya. I also, incidentally, read the first four of Alan Drury's Advise and Consent series which kindled my interest in American politics which, with the arrival of Donald Trump, has become very much stranger than fiction.

My job continued to be as interesting as ever, but having turned down the offer of a partnership I realised that I was getting ready to move on.

I have always been fascinated by the coincidences which shape our lives. Whereas there were tens of thousands of British citizens living in Kenya, including the large communities of Indian origin, there were only a few hundred Danes. The Danish community was quite close-knit, a mixture of families who had arrived in the late 1930s, inspired by Karen Blixen's wonderful book *Out of Africa*, and short-term contract expatriates working mainly in the charity sector. We identified far more closely with the Danish community and I was reasonably fluent in the language. Not long after we returned from leave I was appointed treasurer of the Danish Society in East Africa and it was through my connection with the society that I met, at one of the embassy's social occasions, a visiting Dane, Peter Nienstaedt.

Peter had driven down from Copenhagen in a red Ford Transit camper van, hoping to support himself by freelance journalism. He was writing for a Danish magazine a series of articles entitled *'Paa Feldt Fod genem Afrika'*, which translates roughly as 'Tiptoeing through Africa' – strange what one remembers from some forty years ago. When he eventually ran out of money, being from an advertising background he got a job with Skyline Advertising, an agency owned by an American, Bill Purdy. Bill, who wore a black patch covering his one blind eye, giving him a slightly piratical air, was by then non-executive, and had handed over the running of the agency to another American, Jeff Fulmer, who eventually bought him out.

Peter and I had become friends, Skyline was about to lose its finance director and he introduced me to Jeff as a possible replacement. Jeff took me to dinner, which started with several large martinis mixed in the American way, mostly gin with just the merest hint of vermouth, and made me an offer which appealed to the embryonic entrepreneur in me: he would give me a fixed percentage of the turnover of the company from which I would pay the staff of the accounts department, any surplus being my remuneration.

I was ready to leave the accounting profession, Deloitte agreed not to hold me to my two-year contract and to accept a month's notice. After ten years of enjoyable work as an auditor, the last three in the varied and at times slightly surreal environment of East Africa, I moved on to the next stage of my life.

5. THE LAND

KENYA IS A COUNTRY OF contrasts, a mix of outstanding beauty and raw nature, in places tamed by man into productive farmland, in others an untouched wilderness with endless variations. Within a few hours' drive of Nairobi there are snow-capped mountains, harsh deserts, tropical forests and vast plains teeming with wild animals. There are lakes and waterfalls, caves and active volcanoes, offering so many opportunities for short excursions. Like most expatriate residents we took every opportunity to explore this richness. It was rare to have a weekend when we didn't go somewhere.

In my childhood, television had not been the pervasive influence that it is today but it did serve to introduce me to some of the beauty of nature. I had first seen the variety of East African wildlife through the cameras of Armand and Michaela Denis and the richness of a tropical reef through those of Hans and Lotte Hass, both in hazy black and white. My time in Kenya gave me the opportunity to colour in those memories and to see the vivid reality.

The nearest entrance to the Nairobi National Park was less than half an hour's drive from our flat and we went there often. Its modest 45 square miles were home to large numbers of plains game and all the 'big five' except elephant. There were half a dozen rhino, often seen away from the rough roads, browsing on low bushes. It is tragic to record that poaching reduced the number of black rhinos across Kenya by nearly 98% between 1970 and 1990, from 18,000 to 400. While it was exciting to see them when I was there it was certainly not uncommon. They were always to be found in Amboseli Game Reserve where one of them, named Gertie by the rangers, had a horn more than 4 feet long. One charged me once, in a desultory sort of way, in Tsavo East: he was standing in the road a hundred yards away, I got out of the car to take photos, he picked up my scent, charged in my general direction, then wandered off into the bush.

In all my many drives through the Nairobi Game Park I would find something of interest. I once came across a large python which had just swallowed a small antelope. It was stretched out, unable to move, a few yards in from one of the tracks, an improbably large lump just behind its head. I went back every day for a week and watched the bump get smaller as it travelled down through the animal's digestive system. Another time it was an ostrich nest, the female incubating a dozen or so eggs, which I visited until the chicks were born and I would watch them running round together like a group of tiny ballerinas. There were several cheetah resident in the park and because there were plenty of human visitors they were very used to cars. One year a family of cubs was born, and I often took the short drive to the park for the sheer pleasure of watching them play, with the same exuberance shown by the two small kittens who are playing in the kitchen at Puxley as I write this. They took to jumping up onto people's cars and I recall sitting in my VW Beetle with one on the roof, watching his tail swishing back and forth in front of me like a windscreen wiper.

Not all encounters were quite so benign. A friend stopped his car, a VW Beetle identical to mine, close to the hippo pools on the Athi River at the far end of the park. Hippos graze at night, chomping their way through an amazing 25 kilos of grass daily, and return to the water where they wallow during the day; bizarrely for such a thick-skinned animal they are prone to sunburn. My friend found himself between the water and a late-returning hippo which didn't attempt to skirt his car but took a bite at it, gouging out two long strips of metal with his impressive tusks. Apparently hippos, although not carnivores, kill more people in Africa than any other animal.

I saw my first wild elephant on a drive from Naivasha to Nyeri through the Aberdare Mountains. We were driving through open bush approaching the forest, the air heavy with the scent of the wild sage that grows there, when we saw him, dwarfed by a towering clump of bamboo. The picture is so deep-seated in my memory since that day I have always associated the smell of sage with elephants.

Memories are most vivid when triggered by a smell, a sound or a line in a book. I can be reading, there is a mention of sun-dappled water and suddenly I am sitting with my father-in-law, high up on the banks of the Tana River in Meru National Park, east of Mount Kenya. We have been staying in some self-catering huts, many miles from any other habitation, the only people there. The river is wide, slow and muddy, its banks lush and green fading rapidly to dusty brown away from the water, and the air is crystal clear, every leaf etched onto its branch. It is mid-morning and silent. Africa is noisiest at dusk, night is punctuated by grunts and the occasional howl, but in the heat of the day all is quiet. The sandbanks in the river are littered with crocodiles and the silence is broken only by the blowing of a hippo. I have no words to express the contentment I feel. My father-in-law, Boddy, was one of the most special people in my life and the only one to fully understand my love of Africa.

Another time, another place, another memory, triggered by the damp smell of a forest. We are staying, with friends, in a log-cabin camp 8,000 feet up on the slopes of Mount Kenya. I wake at dawn, go out into the misty morning, dew underfoot, the noise of the river tumbling through the gorge a hundred feet below our little clearing, tangled fig trees towering, protective and unthreatening, above me. I feel alone with the birdsong, my life is in order, I have a small family I adore, I am supremely happy. So much beauty, so much peace, so much excitement, so much fulfillment, so much happiness: is it any wonder my love for Africa is one of the forces that have shaped my life?

Kenya is a fisherman's paradise, with giant Nile perch weighing hundreds of pounds in Lake Turkana, thousand pound plus blue marlin in the Indian Ocean and, in between, brown trout in the mountain streams, catfish in the rivers and black bass and tilapia in the sweet-water lakes of the Rift Valley. My Kenyan fishing memories are of the people I was with and the beauty of the nature around us rather than the catching of fish.

I am not a passionate fisherman, for me fishing has always been about being with friends. I have fond childhood memories of dangling a baited hook in a quiet canal in the Essex countryside, but only so I could spend time uninterrupted with my beloved grandfather; of course we never caught anything. In my early teens I fished for mackerel in the outstandingly beautiful Kenmare estuary, but mackerel fishing could hardly be called sport. Half a dozen feathered hooks were lowered in the water and a couple of minutes later half a dozen beautiful iridescent fish were flopping about in the bottom of the boat. Half an hour later they were our breakfast.

A hundred miles out of Nairobi just off the Mombasa road is Bushwhackers, a camp on the banks of the Galana River. Here the river tumbles over some rapids before curving eastwards to skirt Tsavo Game Park on its way down to meet the Indian Ocean just north of Malindi. At the time the lodge consisted of a handful of basic thatched huts set just back from the river among the acacias, with oil drum barbecues for cooking, long-drop toilets and cold-water showers. It was a place to relax, to wander along the river bank and connect with primal Africa where man is insignificant.

Using bacon rind on a barbed hook we would catch small scavenging catfish, which we smoked in an improvised smoker made from a biscuit tin to render the unappealing flesh almost palatable. Below the rapids herons would stand around in the water waiting to spear the fish as they arrived, stunned by their violent ride down through the rocks. Whitewashed onto the rocks of the far bank were the words 'beware of crocodile', below which we often saw one basking in the afternoon sun. What nearly killed me, however, was not one of the many dangerous animals around but a tiny insect.

Most mosquitoes have front legs longer than the back and, when supping on human blood, stand with their body sloping upwards and their proboscis at a right angle pointing down. The Anopheles, arguably the world's biggest killer and responsible for a million deaths a year from malaria, is unique in that its back legs are higher and its proboscis extends straight out from its body. When it perches on us it becomes a straight and deadly dart, imperceptibly piercing our skin at 45°.

On one of our visits to Bushwhackers, one such mosquito sipped blood from both Bente and me. Ten days later we woke feeling as if we had a hangover, although we had done nothing the previous evening to deserve one. It persisted and we eventually called our doctor, who diagnosed malaria and injected us with appropriate medication. After a couple of days Bente was improving while I was feeling considerably worse. The doctor decided I would be better off in Nairobi hospital where I spent the next couple of weeks. It was, I think, the worst I have ever felt in my life. The symptoms were similar to those of flu magnified many times, with headaches which made any movement impossible and arms and legs constantly aching. I had a high fever, breaking periodically into profuse sweats, and for a while I really did not care whether I lived or died. I had no interest in eating or drinking and was unable to concentrate enough to read but of course I survived, as do most people. On subsequent trips to Bushwhackers we took the appropriate prophylactics.

One of our friends from Parklands, Luigi, a third-generation

Kenyan of Italian descent, had a small fishing lodge on the banks of one of the streams which run down from the Aberdare mountains, irrigating the rich farmlands of the Kinangop before they eventually find their way to Lake Naivasha. We spent a couple of idyllic weekends there with Luigi and other friends, fishing for trout in forests alive with monkeys and parrots. Luigi, an excellent cook, saw the fishing simply as a means of putting food on the table so he baited the river with some pellets made, I believe, from salmon roe. This put the fish into a feeding frenzy so the rest of us could reel them in a little way downstream. Perhaps not sport but we dined well.

The Kenya-born architect of the Holiday Inn project I would pursue for several years, Chris Archer, owned, among his several homes, a large rambling bungalow on the western shore of Lake Naivasha which he once lent us for a weekend. We invited some friends, three couples also with young children and a couple of bachelors. The house sat in the shadow of the Mau escarpment, which rose a couple of thousand feet behind us, and to the right was the distinctive volcanic shape of Mount Longonot. The lakeshore was thick with papyrus and bulrushes, home to a myriad brightly coloured small birds and no doubt a few snakes, but in my experience snakes tend to be shy animals and disappear long before they are seen. There were, fortunately, no crocodiles, crocodiles preferring the warmer waters of lower altitudes. We drove up on the Friday afternoon, had a convivial supper and relaxed evening by a large log fire. Evenings in the uplands of East Africa can be pleasantly cool.

There were several boats, each with its outboard motor, and on the Saturday morning we went out fishing for black bass and tilapia, forcing channels through the floating mats of papyrus to get to the open water. We called a halt when the tally of fish reached 150, more than we could possibly eat. Unfortunately the black bass greatly outnumbered the tilapia; black bass can really only be eaten in a fish pie where their slightly muddy flavour is overpowered by cheese. Tilapia of course have beautiful, clean-tasting, creamy white flesh but they swim deeper than the bass which, greedy as they are, take the spinners long before they reach tilapia depth. Most of the fish finished up with the half-dozen staff who maintained the house. White Kenyans liked to live comfortably.

One of our long-weekend camping trips was to Samburu, north of Mount Kenya. North-eastern Kenya was then and still is wild and largely unregulated, home to *shifta*, bandits who come down from neighbouring Somalia. We drove past Nyeri and Nanyuki, past the entrance to Bob Wilson's estate at Timau and on to Archers Post, where there is a control point. Vehicles are encouraged to stop by a row of spikes across the road and car details are laboriously recorded, although I doubt whether there is any follow-up if they fail to return. We duly stopped, gave our details, watched as the policemen made a great show of hauling the spikes off to one side, drove slowly forward and saw their smiles expand as both nearside tyres blew out on the not-fully-retracted spikes.

'Bwana, that is most unfortunate. Luckily there is a garage just down the road where your tyres can be mended.'

Infuriating, but one of the subtle ways used to redistribute wealth. From then on I always carried two spare wheels.

An hour later, with punctures mended, we drove on into the Samburu Game Reserve and found a beautiful grassy patch beside a small river, fringed with reeds, far from any other habitation. We pitched our tent, made a fire, cooked our dinner, had a few glasses of wine then danced in the moonlight to the music of Ella and Frank and others while our two little girls fell asleep, a magical evening in beautiful country. We were woken the next morning by a warden: 'Bwana, you cannot camp here, too many crocodiles in that river!'

We moved to a less romantic but safer place for the second night.

I spent another weekend camping in Samburu, this time with Don Blacklaw, a client who had become a friend. We met at his lovely rambling house on the shore of lake Naivasha and drove in convoy over the Aberdare Mountains to Nyeri and on through Archers Post to Buffalo Springs where, we found a similar camping spot beside a river, a tributary of the Uaso Nyiro. Don liked to camp in comfort and had brought his cook along with him. The following day was Sunday, we had a full English breakfast, always good when eaten in the open air by a campfire and absolutely best when that campfire is by a river on the plains of East Africa.

Don and I, both short-sighted, left our spectacles on the river bank and washed ourselves in the shallow water, ducking under the surface to rinse the dust of Africa out of our hair. We dressed and went in my car for a game drive, leaving the cook to prepare a traditional lunch of roast beef. On our return a couple of hours later we found the coo, not, as we'd hoped, busy around the fire with the roast potatoes crisping up and the beef resting but cowering in the back of Don's large old station waggon.

'*Wapi chakula?* Where's lunch?' asked Don, in puzzlement, not anger.

'Oh bwana, just after you left a big crocodile he come out of the bushes and into the river and he wouldn't go away.'

We had lunch at the nearby Samburu Lodge.

A couple of years later I took my father-in-law on a similar camping trip, minus of course the cook. I greatly enjoyed Boddy's company. He was more a father to me than my own ever was, and on his annual visits to Kenya he and I always went off for a long weekend to one or other of the game parks. In earlier years we had been to lush Tsavo, dry and dusty Amboseli and remote Meru. This time I wanted to show him Samburu, which had become one of my favourites.

We had a long and dusty drive from Nairobi and stopped for a swim at Buffalo Springs, now hardly more than a walled well but at the time a large, deep, clear and inviting pool and a regular stopping-off point for travellers on the way north to Marsabit. We stripped off, removed our glasses, waded in and within a couple of yards were out of our depth in beautiful cool water, splashing around like a couple of schoolboys, revelling in being together once more in Africa – to both of us Africa was this, life in the rawness of nature not the comfortable suburbs of Nairobi. Eventually we got out and as we reclaimed our glasses we looked up and saw a small family of elephants ambling down the low ridge just the other side of the water, intent on having their early-evening drink. I sometimes wonder how they, and indeed we, would have reacted had we still been in the middle of the pool. Many years later, at the family dinner to celebrate his seventy-fifth birthday Boddy formally thanked me for those times in Africa: in his words, 'Those were the best years of my life.'

When Marina was six one of her school friends was picnicking with his parents beside Buffalo Springs. The boy wandered a little way off to explore the marshy run-off, where the overflow from the spring-fed pool trickled away to the nearby Uaso Nyiro, when an 8 foot crocodile emerged, grabbed him and started to drag him back towards the water. The parents, powered by adrenaline, gave chase; the father straddled the beast and managed to lever open its jaw while the mother pulled the boy out. The flying doctor was called and the child was taken straight to Nairobi hospital. He was given 160 stitches and left with scarred tooth-marks which no doubt gave him serious bragging rights for the rest of his life.

I look back on those magical adventures and am tempted to say, like Boddy, 'Those were the best years of my life.' Getting closer to the end of my life, though, I think that the life I am living right now is, in its rather more mellow way, as good as it's ever been.

6. THE MOUNTAINS

I HAVE LOVED MOUNTAINS SINCE I first saw the Swiss Alps at the age of nine. A strong childhood memory is the excitement of going on my first skiing holiday, waking before dawn on the train from Calais to Chur, lying on my upper bunk gazing out at the first mountains I had ever seen as the rolling green of the Jura gradually gave way to the snow of the Alps. That memory has been supplemented and made more powerful by my memories of East Africa's snow-capped giants and, much later in my life, the Himalayas.

A dozen miles to the west of Nairobi, prominent on the skyline, lie the Ngong Hills – 'hills' in East Africa but, at two and a half thousand metres, more than twice the height of any mountain in the UK. Karen Blixen's beautiful Out of Africa, one of the books which drew me to Africa, begins 'I had a farm in Africa at the foot of the Ngong Hills.' Her lover Denys Finch Hatton is buried near the top of those hills, in a place of her choosing. He was a hunter who loved animals, and it is said that for years after his death lions would come at sunset and sit on his grave, which carries a simple inscription from The Rime of the Ancient Mariner: 'He prayeth well, who loveth well both man and bird and beast'. I had greatly enjoyed Blixen's book and a visit to her lover's grave was one of our first trips out of Nairobi. We saw no lions but there was, at least, a herd of buffalo grazing a few hundred yards away. It became a regular picnic spot for us.

Mount Kenya rises jagged from the dusty plains and marks the boundary between the settled and civilised farmland to the south and west and the wilder land of nomads and shifta to the north and east. Its two highest peaks, Batian and Nelian, are only climbed by serious mountaineers but the third peak, Point Lenana, a whisker under 5,000 metres above sea level, was the culmination of a trek, albeit a very testing one, which I did in 1971 with three friends. We spent the night before at Naro Moru River Lodge, had an excellent dinner by a large log fire and made an early start the next day.

After a substantial breakfast we were driven up through the forest till the track petered out at a little over 2,000 metres. Here we started our trek. The first mile or so was through dense woodlands, huge ficus trees draped with lianas, once the hiding place of Mau Mau terrorists and now a protected nature reserve home to elephant, buffalo and lions, which of course remained hidden. Like most animals they sensibly try to avoid man. The trees gave way first to towering bamboo then at about 3,000 metres to moorland, and in front of us was the fabled 'vertical bog'. Vertical is of course an exaggeration, but it was steep and inexplicably remained sodden in spite of its 45° gradient.

It was a slow and muddy trudge up, almost impossible without climbing poles. At the top was a large cave where we caught our breath before heading off to the left, on a gentler gradient up to the apex of a ridge. Ahead of us was the Teleki Valley, an idyllic pathway to the peaks. The valley was lush and green, and home to the extraordinary plants and flowers that have evolved under its unique conditions of cool high altitude and long hours of equatorial sunshine, fed by glacier meltwaters. Giant lobelias and groundsel not found anywhere else on the planet, rich feeding stations for a myriad humming birds and sunbirds, were dotted around in the moorland with peat-brown streams threading through them and, apart from a hut and a couple of permanent tented camps, little impact from humans. In the course of our three-day trip we did not see another person. We settled into the Teleki hut where we were to spend the night; it had basic furniture, eight or ten bunk beds, a table and a few chairs and, in one corner looking slightly incongruous, an old pair of wooden skis, presumably abandoned years earlier by a rather ambitious climber.

We relaxed in the cool, late afternoon sunshine while our two guides prepared a simple stew. A stream ran close to the tent, its water stained brown by the peat it ran through. It combined beautifully with the whisky from the small flask I had brought, one of the two luxuries I had permitted myself, rucksack weight being important; the other was of course a book. We ate early and slept the sleep of contented exhaustion.

The next morning two of us set off up the valley with one of the guides, the other two choosing for their own reasons to simply explore the valley. It was a long and gradual uphill walk beside the stream, the well-worn path threading its way through the towering lobelias, and we walked in silence, slightly overawed by the jagged peaks of Batian and Nelian with their tumbling rock faces to our left and the equally forbidding Point John straight ahead, separated from the higher peaks by the Lewis glacier. By comparison our objective, Point Lenana, slightly to our right, looked for all the world like the gentle nursery slopes in the Alps where I had learnt to ski twenty years earlier, a shining white dome of snow.

Looks can be deceptive. It was steeper than it appeared from a distance and we climbed with ice axes, digging out steps in the hard-frozen snow, straining for each cold and painful breath in the thin atmosphere, our aching muscles crying out for what little oxygen such breaths contained. The last couple of hundred metres was among the toughest physical tests of my life, three painful steps up, a pause for breath while slowly slipping back, repeat and repeat and repeat. But eventually we made it: a huge sense of achievement, the effort completely justified by beauty almost beyond words, the forbidding peaks towering over us 500 metres to our north and the endless plains of Africa to the south. Mount Kilimanjaro, more than 200 miles away, was just visible in the crystal clear and unpolluted atmosphere.

After taking the obligatory photographs we allowed ourselves an exhilarating sleigh ride back down on our bottoms, descending the thousand feet to the valley in a few glorious minutes. We walked back to Mackinder's Camp, where we were to spend the second night in tents before descending back to Naro Moru. After a light lunch I was lying in my open tent, my hands clasped on my stomach, dozing contentedly, when I felt something on my hand. I opened my eyes to see that a small bird had come into the tent, perched on my thumb and was looking at me, his head cocked to one side; after a few seconds he decided that I was of no great interest and flew back out into the open air. I had with me a simple guide to the birds of East Africa and there he was, on the page devoted to the mountains, the mountain chat whose only notable characteristic was a complete fearlessness of man.

We spent a quiet evening and after dinner, as the temperature fell below freezing, I sat by the large log fire re-living the climb and finishing off the last of my whisky. The following morning we walked back down to Naro Moru River Lodge, taking a few hours to slither down the vertical bog and stroll back along the forest paths.

I look back on the climb as a considerable achievement, but reading No Picnic on Mount Kenya by Felice Benuzzi tempers my pride. During the Second World War there was a prison camp near Nanyuki housing Italian prisoners of war captured in nearby Ethiopia and Somalia. By all accounts they were a pleasant and relaxed group of men, many of whom stayed on in Kenya at after the war. Apparently three of them, seeing the magnificent mountain as the backdrop to their captivity, decided they had to climb it.

They spent six months planning the climb, making crampons and ice axes from scrap metal scavenged from around the camp, ropes by unravelling the bases of their Indian-style beds, makeshift tents and warm clothing from blankets. One evening, at the end of their shift working in the camp's vegetable patch, they slipped off into the bush and headed for the mountain. Lacking detailed knowledge of the proven routes Batian proved to be beyond them, but they did reach the top of Point Lenana where they planted a home-made Italian flag. Fifteen days after their escape they sneaked back into the camp, to the surprise of their fellow inmates who assumed they had made their way back to Somalia a couple of hundred miles to the north-east.

Towards the end of my time in Kenya I got to know the Assistant Commissioner of Lands, Frank Charnley, who was a keen mountaineer. Years earlier, he had spent a couple of weeks of his local leave wandering round the glaciers of the mountain and had an article on them published in a mountaineering magazine. To his great surprise he thus became a world expert on equatorial glaciers, a field in which there is little competition.

Some years later, with a few friends from Round Table, I reached the summit of Africa's highest mountain, Kilimanjaro. Again it was a long hard trek rather than a climb. Kilimanjaro, Kili to those who've climbed it, is the highest free-standing mountain in the world, a dormant volcano rising 5,000 metres from the surrounding plains. It has two peaks; to the west is Kibo, a picture-book snow-capped volcanic crater with its rim intact, and to the east Mawenzi, the jagged heart of a worn-down caldera. From a distance it is beautiful, with its shining white snow cap above the grey of its scree and the vivid green of its forests. Up close it is magnificent; breathtakingly lovely.

At the time I wrote an account for the Round Table newsletter, which I reproduce verbatim in spite of my slight embarrassment at what is now to me the rather juvenile humour:

KLIVES'S KILIMANJARO KLIMB
by Sherpa ben-Samuel

22.1.75

15.20 hours. *Depart from May and Baker to the cheering of crowds of faithful employees – Colin Robson and two messengers (Lavita was attending to her eye make-up).*

15.35 hours. *Return to May and Baker to collect Clive's passport.*

20.00 hours. *Arrived Marangu Hotel. Proprietress looks us over, tells Clive and me that we had better have the bridal suite, but must be ready for dinner by 8.30. Hotel brochure boasts a 'varied menu with a continental touch'. Dinner, posho with garlic. Waiter informs us that bread is eaten with breakfast, not dinner. Clive takes all the hot water for his bath, last time I share a bridal suite with him.*

23.1.75

07.30 hours. *Breakfast, polenta Hawaiian (uji with pineapple) fried egg with liver (bacon's off, love, this is Tanzania).*

08.30 hours. *Ready to depart on the great climb.*

11.00 hours. *Departed. Seven of us carrying three ten-pound haversacks between us, eleven porters carrying forty pounds each. After two hours easy walk Chairman Clive, on the point of collapse, passes his haversack to the nearest porter. (To be fair I also heave a sigh of relief as I was sharing the haversack with him.)*

16.00 hours. *Arrive at first hut, 9000 ft. exhausted.*

Major discoveries – a) that our guide, Faustino, is a passable cook, b) that lime flavoured Fizzy tablets dissolved in muddy brown water is probably the most revolting looking drink ever.

19.30 hours. *Lulled to sleep by the gentle sounds of two Italian men trying to seduce two young American girls in the room next door and Chairman Clive moaning with jealousy .*

24.1.75

06.30 hours. *Photographed sunrise(!), excellent breakfast.*

08.00 hours. *Set off for second hut. Met many tourists coming down - question - Why were all Germans, both going up and down, miserable? Are they forced to go up? (Ve haff ways of making you climb!) (Sincere apologies to Ziggy and Volkmer.)*

14.00 *Arrived at second hut, 12,350', after a ten mile walk. Our afternoon nap was disturbed by the sound of a Toyota Land Cruiser arriving. Chairman Clive was forcibly restrained from hitching a lift back down. Colin Robson prefers Fizzy tablets to whisky – must be a foreigner - sounds like one in any case. Nothing to seduce so asleep by 19.30 hours.*

25/1/75

06.30 hours. *Breakfast followed by a combined effort to convert the long-drop to a short-drop. Walked to Kibo hut, 15,000', 10 miles across high moorland and windswept desert; the cold and the altitude become very evident. A light supper and in bed by six o'clock. Only Peter Middleton sleeps but John Broadhead still manages to snore in my left ear.*

26.1.75

00.45 hours. *Awakened by Faustino. ¼" of snow has fallen, the moon is nearly full, there is no wind and the stars are brighter than anyone thought possible, the whole scene indescribable.*

01.30 hours. *Began to climb the frozen scree, guides with paraffin lamps going first and last. We moved at a snail's pace full of apprehension, one thought in all our minds - "what the hell am I doing here?".*

07.00 hours. *Arrived at Gilman's Point, on the rim of the crater, the top of the mountain, just after the sun rose behind Mawenzi. Disappointingly not the best sunrise I have ever seen, however, I got a photograph for my grandchildren. Set off for Uhuru peak, a two mile walk and 500' climb round the crater's rim.*

Clive and Colin Taylor fell victim to altitude sickness part of the way round and were taken back by a guide. For the honour of No.1 I continued, prepared to place our banner on Uhuru Peak, only to find that Clive had taken it back down with him. John Broadhead and Peter Middleton arrived fresh as daisies (sorry, Duckies).

Colin Robson had to be shaken awake after every stop but got there and Eric Cook in spite of acute nausea reached the peak, looking like death warmed up.

08.30 hours. *Set off back down - one hour to Gilman's Point, one hour back to Kibo hut, a rest and then two hours back to second hut. In bed, whacked, by seven o'clock.*

27.1.75

Breakfast at 06.30 hours. Why did young couple from hut next door go to the long-drop together? Another first for the Guinness Book of records? 20 miles back to Marangu Hotel before lunch, and so to Nairobi.

To summarize: a long and very pleasant walk followed by a hell of a climb. Moments of boredom, moments of agony and moments of unbelievable beauty; a feeling of anticlimax at the summit ("God, this is an awful place" would have been appropriate, if unoriginal), and a feeling of achievement when it was all over; and throughout first class fellowship.'

I had quite forgotten writing this account until it was sent to me by one of my fellow climbers, Colin Taylor, who in one of life's strange coincidences lives in Farnham a couple of hundred yards from the house we moved into when we returned to the UK. I had already written a description from memory, which I found was wrong in a couple of key details. In my memory we had a guide and a couple of porters – forgetting that it takes a small army to carry all the food, water and firewood for five days. I had also forgotten that the two members of our party with whom I remain in contact did not make the summit.

That article was brief, the Round Table newsletter not being a lengthy publication, so I will add some details which are deeply etched into my memory.

When we met with our guides and porters in the forest clearing where we left our cars it was apparent that, while we had decent climbing boots and warm clothing (although to my enduring embarrassment I started the climb in purple flares), they mostly wore quite skimpy clothes and tackies, the ubiquitous gym shoes of the day. As we were to find out this didn't stop them making the five-day trek look effortless while being both encouraging and sympathetic to us as we struggled with the increasing altitude.

The first day was all in thick and lush rain forest. There was steady drizzle and it was gloomy under the thick canopy high above. We wound our way up the mountain's gentle lower slopes, the paths, criss-crossed with tree roots, made treacherous by running water, and we were muddy and exhausted by the time we reached Mandara Hut. We washed off the worst of the mud in the stream running past the hut, and relaxed in the warmth of the late afternoon – I still have photos.

On the second day we soon emerged from the forest onto open moorland and after an hour or so we got our first glimpse of Kibo with its shining mantle of snow, far more extensive than it is now. It was to loom above us for the next couple of days. We had a glorious few hours' walk, made easier by having our objective always in sight, even though tantalisingly it did not appear to get any nearer. We spent the night at Horombo, a small group of huts larger than Mandara as it accommodated climbers returning from the top as well as those on their way up.

Day three was the day of high-altitude desert. We quickly reached the saddle between Mawenzi and Kibo and for six monotonous hours we trudged across gravel and scree, the only plant life surviving huddled in what little wind-shelter there was. By the last hour the slopes had become significantly steeper, and it was a relief to reach Kibo Hut, perched on the exposed southern flank of the peak towering steeply above us. We were by then at 4,700 metres above sea level, as high as Mont Blanc, the highest mountain in Western Europe, were gasping for breath and looking with real trepidation at the mass of Kibo, rising sharply a couple of hundred metres away from the already steep slope. The forest below us was now shrouded in cloud, the jagged peak of Mawenzi a few miles away etched razor sharp against the eastern horizon.

We ate a light meal at six and the guides insisted we then try to sleep: we had to start our final climb just after midnight in order to reach the rim of the crater by sunrise, not for the fabulous sight of the day dawning over Mawenzi but because it is far easier to climb the scree before the sun has melted the ice which binds it together.

We slept little, emerging from our sleeping bags at the

scheduled time and forcing ourselves to eat the porridge cooked up by our guides. I said in my light-hearted article that the whole scene was 'indescribable', but it is so firmly etched onto my memory that I will try to do so.

The light dusting of snow was glittering in the light of the nearly full moon. The stars didn't twinkle (they need some air pollution to do that) but shone out with quite unexpected brilliance, and it was one of the most beautiful sights of my life. I stood looking south over the vast plains of Africa, their blackness only broken by a few pinpricks where log fires burned, the great canopy of stars overhead stretching from horizon to horizon and it was, in the truest sense of the word, utterly awesome: I can see it in my memory as clearly today as I did nearly fifty years ago.

At midnight we set off in single file, one of the guides leading the way, another at the back to give gentle encouragement whenever we slowed. From the base of the great crater above us we made long sweeping traverses, digging our boots into the frozen scree, a few steps at a time, each step an achievement. The climb seemed interminable but eventually, after six hours of laboriously placing one foot in front of the other, we staggered over the ridge of Gilman's Point and flopped down onto the deep snow which softened the rim of the crater.

Dawn had lightened the sky and I took photos of the sun rising behind Mawenzi. I could only change lenses and load film by removing my gloves and the temperature was well below freezing. With the added wind-chill factor of the strong breeze I only had seconds before the cold numbed my fingers, but the resulting few pictures, which of course I still treasure, are worth every bit of discomfort.

From then on I found it a comparatively easy stroll around the rim of the crater. Inside, a hundred or so metres below us and stark against the deep white snow was a small figure-of-eight shaped patch of bare black rock, evidence of the volcanic heat still simmering deep down; molten rock had last erupted as lava from the side of the mountain only a few hundred years ago. Two members of the group were stricken with altitude sickness but five of us made it to Uhuru Peak, the highest point in Africa, and in my quiet competitiveness I increased my pace to make sure I got there first. That throughout the climb I did not suffer from any of the usual effects of high altitude was purely down to luck. The one who suffered most was the fittest among us, a seriously dedicated rugby-playing sportsman.

For the past few years I had looked up at this amazingly beautiful mountain, wondering what it would be like to climb it: now I knew.

After we had enjoyed our feeling of achievement and the obligatory photographs had been taken, we set off down, which was considerably easier than going up. The warmth of the sun had thawed the frozen slopes and what had taken six hours to climb took less than half an hour of joyful scree-running to get down. We had a quick second breakfast at the Kibo hut then carried straight on to Horombo where we spent the night.

The next day we walked back over the moorland and through the forest, thankful that the rain had stopped, getting back to our cars by lunchtime. To thank our guides, who had been excellent, kind when we needed sympathy, cajoling when we needed encouragement, and unfailingly cheerful, we gave them our climbing boots and some of our warm clothing. Whether they ever wore them we will never know: they seemed quite comfortable in their worn out clothes and gym shoes. Rather than stay another night in Moshi we drove the six hours back to Nairobi, arriving back exhausted and happy.

Twenty-five years later I repeated the climb, this time with my daughter Emma. She was nineteen, the youngest in our mixed group of seventeen people; I was the oldest, in my late fifties. The changes brought about by the growth in international tourism were huge. What had been rutted little tracks through the forest had become well-worn paths, the camps had grown from single huts to large encampments, and we were hardly ever out of sight of other parties. The biggest change was at Horombo, where walkers stay both going up and coming down: it had become a well-organised circle of A-frame timber huts accommodating 300 climbers, and the kitchen area was swarming with ravens scavenging among the food scraps.

At Kibo hut we met an English father and son who, quite bizarrely, performed a Morris dance in full traditional costume. It was their ambition, they told us, to do the highest-altitude Morris dance ever. They probably succeeded, and in doing so reaffirmed my opinion of Morris dancers. They did not go on up to the summit. I assume they were in a hurry to head down for a few well-earned pints of bitter.

All the increased facilities did not of course make the climb any easier. I was twenty years older than anyone else in our group and on the final morning, when the seven of us who attempted the summit were climbing the scree, I struggled to keep up. Every time a brief five-minute rest was called I would have fallen behind by about five minutes, so by the time I caught up with the others they were about to move on. Emma tried her best both to get them to wait a little longer and to encourage me by holding out tempting tablets of glucose, but time was too important: it was essential to reach the top of the scree before sunrise. When we reached Gilman's Point I decided to stay there while the others went on to the summit. The sun came up on schedule and it was good to be able to take a series of photos in the rapidly changing light. After half an hour or so I went back down to Kibo hut, treading carefully as my ankles no longer had the suppleness to cushion the joyful scree-running of my earlier climb, rejoined those who had remained there and enjoyed a leisurely breakfast.

The man-made changes on the mountain were superficial against the vast backdrop of nature, but the changes caused by man's profligate use of resources were not: the snow cap had shrunk noticeably during the twenty-three years between my climbs and I read recently that it will disappear completely within the next ten years. The snows of Kilimanjaro, backdrop to the memories of Hemingway's dying hero, will be gone for ever.

We completed the climb on 12 July, the day of the final of the 1998 football World Cup. The small motel where we were staying had no television, but our guides located a house which did. It was about 5 miles out of town with no immediate neighbours; the owner had equipped it as an unofficial bar and was happy for us to watch the match there. We all piled into the back of a pickup truck which our guides had acquired somewhere, standing packed like vertical sardines, reached the large bungalow without mishap, and spent the evening relaxing from the climb and drinking beer while watching what I remember as a rather boring match.

Mount Kenya and Kilimanjaro are towering and impressive, dominating the landscape, but there are lesser mountains which we also enjoyed climbing. Among them was the dormant volcano Mount Longonot, which rises from the floor of the Rift Valley a few miles south of Lake Naivasha and was a favourite place for a weekend picnic. At its base was a large cave, home to a colony of bats and carpeted by guano. There was a well-worn path round the mountain which took us to the rim of the crater in an hour or so, and in the crater itself at nearby Hell's Gate there were fissures from which wisps of steam emerged, a reminder that the volcano was dormant, not extinct.

Mountains have a way of putting our puny lives into perspective. To stand on the top of a high mountain is to feel the insignificance of the achievements of our own civilization and to be in awe of the wonders of creation, whether or not one believes in a god as the creator or, as I do, in the primal forces of nature doing their own creation. It is also easy to understand why many early civilizations believed that their gods dwelt on mountain tops. I feel closest to the powers that control our destiny when standing on top of a mountain.

7. THE COAST

THE IMMENSITY OF THE INDIAN Ocean is almost beyond comprehension. It covers more than 25 million square miles, nearly 20% of the surface of the planet. If you were to stand on the beach at Diani facing east-south-east, between you and Western Australia more than 5,000 miles away there would be nothing but the Indian Ocean. Since first looking out over its blue-grey vastness in 1968 I have been fortunate enough to get to know a few of its myriad small islands: I have visited Zanzibar, Madagascar and Mafia Island, holidayed in the Maldives, Sri Lanka and Mauritius and swum in the warm waters of the Lakshadweep Islands and the Comoro Islands as well as the decidedly cooler waters of Rottnest Island off the coast of Perth. I have spent lazy hours drifting over its coral reefs; I have enjoyed the company of sharks, turtles, dolphins and stingrays and sat on the sea floor twenty metres down watching a manta perform her beautiful underwater ballet.

My parents-in-law timed their first visit to Kenya to coincide with the two weeks local leave to which I was entitled to after one year's service. We arranged to spend a week at the coast with them, stopping for a couple of nights in Tsavo West National park on the way back. It was our first visit to the coast and, being on a limited budget, we had rented a self-catering cottage on Diani beach, 20 or so miles south of Mombasa. Looking back, having got used to the luxury of modern estate cars, I am amazed that five of us plus luggage managed to squeeze into our little VW Beetle. My father-in-law was a large man, my wife was heavily pregnant with our second child and we also had to take with us essential foodstuffs, having no idea what would be available locally.

We left our little flat before dawn and were on the Mombasa road before there was any traffic. Somewhere past Athi River the sun rose over the eastern horizon ahead of us, the road dipped quite sharply and the sun disappeared, to appear again as we crested the next rise. My mother-in-law, who was later diagnosed as bipolar, was so taken with the beauty of the landscape and the double sunrise that she insisted we stop the car so she could dance in the middle of the road in the early morning sunlight.

There were at the time three regular stopping points in the 300 miles from Nairobi to Mombasa, Hunters Lodge a hundred miles south of Nairobi, Tsavo Inn 50 miles of mostly unmade road further on and Voi Lodge after another 50. There was nowhere to stop in the final hundred miles, most of which was scrubby bush and arid desert. We had breakfast at Hunters Lodge before tackling the rocky 35 miles of unmade road, including a couple of tricky dongas which severely tested the suspension of the overloaded VW, and it was a relief to reach the calm oasis of Tsavo Inn knowing that we were halfway, and that all the rest of the journey to Mombasa would be on good tarmac road.

Tsavo Inn was a low, rambling lodge shaded by acacias with great clusters of weaverbird nests hanging like some strange fruit. The gardens were a riot of colour, a mass of frangipani and poinsettias, with bougainvillea draped everywhere. We had a second breakfast, my in-laws' first experience of the delights of a plateful of tropical fruits, pawpaw, mangoes and passion fruit then being almost unknown in northern Europe.

Before setting off again Boddy and I refuelled and checked the car at the service station next door – we had descended nearly 3,000 feet from Nairobi and the tyre pressures were significantly down. Wandering around the service area we saw our first goliath beetles.

Between Tsavo Inn and Voi we saw a small family of elephants browsing on the bushes beside the road, the first wild elephants my in-laws had seen. We watched them for a while, keeping our engine running just in case they got curious about us but they were, of course, quite unconcerned. They were used to traffic on the road and we were no threat.

During the rest of our time in Kenya we drove that road many times and it was rare not to see elephant somewhere in the fifty miles between Tsavo and Voi. The 9,000 square miles of Tsavo which borders the road on either side was home at the time to a fluctuating population of between 10,000 and 25,000 elephants. Having no natural predators apart from man, the population would grow until the vegetation could not support them and they had to be culled to prevent mass starvation. Sadly, since then poaching has kept numbers down, the only positive being that there is now enough food for all. In spite of the poaching Tsavo is still one of the best places on the planet to watch these beautiful beasts in their natural habitat. Successive Kenyan governments have done a wonderful job in setting aside huge areas for wildlife. To give an idea of the scale, if a line were drawn from Southampton on the south coast of England up to the city of Oxford 65 miles to the north, then 100 miles east to the Essex coast near Chelmsford, the area enclosed, the entire south-east of England, home to more than 15 million people, is slightly less than the size of Tsavo. Tsavo itself is not the largest game reserve in East Africa: the Selous reserve in Tanzania is more than double the size.

In the 100 miles from Voi to Mombasa sisal plantations gradually gave way to the Taru desert, an arid area of dense thorn bushes which for more than 300 years proved an impenetrable barrier to European exploration and exploitation. Approaching Mombasa the desert in turn gave way to settlement and we could feel the rapid rise in humidity and enjoy our first sight of the lushness of coastal vegetation.

We stopped in the old city, with its chaotic mix of Portuguese, Arabic and African architecture, to buy the perishables which would not have survived the eight-hour drive in an overcrowded and non-air-conditioned little car. Mombasa is an island, connected to the mainland in the west by a causeway and in the north by the Nyali Bridge, from which the road heads up to Malindi and Lamu. The road south was reached by a ferry plying constantly across the mouth of the busy Mombasa harbour, only half a mile wide but deep and not worth the considerable expense of building a bridge.

The last 20 miles were on smooth sand through orderly plantations of elegant coconut palms, whose fronds dappled the road with sunlight. On either side we caught tantalizing glimpses of the ocean, grey in the late afternoon light. When we finally reached our destination, Mrs May's cottages, and had our first sight of the white sand beach and the Indian Ocean in all its immensity, our tiredness and the stresses imposed by the journey were forgotten. Our cottage was one of seven, simple but idyllic, sitting part-way up the side of a shallow natural amphitheatre among the palms and the casuarinas with the beach a few paces away. The sea was warm and fishermen wandered along the beach selling their catch for almost nothing, a live lobster costing seven shillings, at the time equivalent to one dollar. There was fresh fruit in abundance, mangoes and papayas straight from the tree, whole baskets of oranges for a few shillings.

At the time mass tourism to East Africa was only just beginning, intercontinental air travel being prohibitively expensive, and there were only a handful of hotels on the entire coast. Nyali Beach Hotel, north of Mombasa, was the largest, with Ocean Sport at Watamu, Lawfords, the Blue Marlin and a couple more in Malindi. The biggest on Diani Beach was

Two Fishes, which later became a favourite, but our budget was tight, Mrs May's cottages were strongly recommended by colleagues, and as Kenya residents it somehow seemed more appropriate to stay somewhere simple and self-catering. We had a wonderfully relaxing few days, only slightly marred by Mormor being bitten by one of the ubiquitous monkeys when she didn't feed it. At low tide we waded out to the reef and explored its rich biodiversity; at other times we swam, took long walks along the almost empty beach or relaxed reading in the shade of the palms. I do not recall snorkelling – that came later. Mormor did the cooking, lobsters a couple of evenings, otherwise fish and vegetables and fruit bought from vendors who called in daily.

On the way back we broke our journey for a couple of nights in Tsavo West, staying at Kitani Lodge, also recommended by colleagues – our budget wouldn't run to Kilaguni. We were visited during the night by an elephant which chewed a little at the palm frond roof and, finding it not to his liking, ambled off. My mother-in-law did not particularly enjoy the experience; my father-in-law, like me, fell in love with Africa and from then on they returned every year.

After that first trip we went back to the coast many times and my memories are almost all good. Our closest friends, Hans-Eric Borgholm, chief engineer at East African Portland Cement, and his wife Irma, invited us several times to his company's beach house at Kikambala, 20 miles north of Mombasa. It was just north of Mtwapa Creek, which at the time was crossed by a rusty old ferry taking half a dozen cars. The ferry was propelled by a gang of men hauling a chain laid on the bed of the creek. They would hoist it, dripping and weed-bedecked, onto their shoulders and walk the 40 feet from bow to stern before dropping it and returning to join the back of the gang, singing rhythmically, their beautiful bass voices in time with their steady march. There was usually a wait of 15 minutes or so and while waiting we would buy a fresh coconut from one of the vendors working the queue, who would lop the top off with a panga. For reasons I don't understand the milk was always refreshingly cool in spite of the 35 degree heat of the coast.

The beach house was a large four-bedroom bungalow, thatched with *makuti*, which sat unobtrusively in a five-acre plot in a palm grove a few yards back from the white sand beach. There were no immediate neighbours and it was rare to see another person on the beach. Between the beach and the reef a couple of hundred yards offshore, the water was fairly shallow, only good for swimming at high tide; around low tide it was easy to wade out to the reef which we often did, usually picking up one or two of the countless cowrie shells – at the time we did not realise how delicately balanced the complex ecosystem of the reef was.

I have powerful memories of our first visit to Kikambala. Margaret was a few months old and one morning she woke crying. The house had thin walls and to stop her waking the others I wrapped myself in a kikoi, gathered her up in the crook of my arm, collected my camera and went outside. As we walked through the palm trees towards the beach the sun rose over the ocean, I lifted the camera and snapped. It isn't a brilliant photo but I treasure it for the memories it brings back, memories of being with good friends in Africa, by the Indian Ocean with my second child, calm now, snuggled against my bare chest.

Later that day Bente and Hans had gone to the local *duka* for some supplies, taking Marina with them. Irma and I were sitting on a bench at the top of the beach with Margaret in a carry-cot close to my feet, when Irma jumped onto the bench and, speechless, pointed at the nearby bushes. A large black mamba, fully two metres long, had emerged and was heading for us. I stayed absolutely still, not because I thought it was the right thing to do but in the temporary petrification of sheer terror: the snake slithered between my feet and the carrycot in which my baby daughter was sleeping, a gap of no more than eighteen inches, then disappeared back into the bushes. It took a while for my heartbeat to return to normal.

On one of our trips down to Kikambala we made a detour off the main road to buy provisions. The family remained in the car while I called in to a small and dimly lit duka. Inside, a young African woman, traditionally dressed in black with a cotton shawl covering her head but not her face, was chatting casually to the shopkeeper. It was rare for a European to visit such places; on seeing me she immediately snatched up the end of her shawl and lifted it to cover her face, in doing so revealing her breasts and I thought, how different are our cultural priorities. Another time, driving up to Kikambala we saw, beside the long and dusty road, a solitary lavatory pan in a fetching shade of pink, unconnected to anything around. If it fell off the back of a lorry it did so gently, being quite un-chipped and in pristine condition; I suspect there was a story but will never know it: just one of Africa's small mysteries.

Another time, driving alone from Mombasa to Watamu, I came up behind a young African laboriously peddling his bicycle with a hammerhead shark lashed over the back wheel, one of those little African vignettes which stick in the memory. It was further up the road towards Malindi that I first saw a camel in the back of a pick-up truck, an extraordinary sight at the time but a decade or so later, when I had become a regular visitor to the Arabian Gulf, quite common.

The last time we stayed in the idyllic house at Kikambala was shortly before Hans and Irma were due to return to Denmark. The final evening the four of us sat on the beach, smoking pot and eating roast chicken as we watched the moon rise, perform a small semicircle and set again. It was an emotional time – they had become good friends and to my surprise Irma told me privately that her greatest regret at leaving would be no longer seeing me. When we took them to the airport for their flight back to Denmark she handed me a large package, explaining that they had used an unexpected tax refund to buy me a gift: when we got home I unwrapped a Pentax Spotmatic, my first single-lens reflex camera. The camera still works and

I have and treasure the receipt, for 1270 Ksh, £63 at the time, from Nilestar Cameras.

On one trip to the coast we were in a small motor launch in Mombasa harbour, for reasons I cannot now recall, when a sailing dinghy capsized close by. We took it in tow and the couple who had been sailing it joined us in the launch. As we motored back through the harbour, which is extensive with the port on the north side and mangroves and palm groves to the south, Marina, aged three or four, always inquisitive, asked a steady stream of questions: 'Daddy, what's that?' 'Why is that there?' 'What is that for?'

After a while the man, whose jaw had been slowly dropping, asked 'is she always like this?' and I told him of course she was. To me, a fairly new father, this was normal, how does a child learn if not by asking questions? Over the years, though, I realised that she was unusually inquisitive, which perhaps explains why as an adult she has such a wide range of interests and skills, from composing music to writing mobile phone apps to tiling a bathroom.

It was towards the end of our time in Kenya that I learnt to scuba dive. We had fallen in love with snorkelling, particularly round the large coral heads in the deep water inside the reef at Watamu, a little south of Ocean Sport Hotel, which became our favourite place to stay at the coast after the departure of Hans and Irma. These coral heads remained submerged at low tide when the water was smooth and were home to huge numbers of brilliantly coloured small reef fish as well as a couple of groupers so large that they could no longer emerge from the holes in which they lurked. It was, incidentally, snorkelling at Watamu which persuaded me to give up smoking: I was swimming off a small boat, drifting lazily over the reefs, lost in the beauty of the underwater world when I felt the usual craving for nicotine (I was then smoking twenty or so cigarettes a day). It drove me to haul myself out of the water into the boat and light up a slightly soggy cigarette. I sat there watching the snorkels of my friends while puffing on something which I knew had the potential to kill me, and realised that my habit was powerful enough to stop doing one of the things I loved most so I could satisfy the tobacco craving. A few days later, back in Nairobi, I woke up and decided that from then on I was a non-smoker. I haven't had a cigarette since, apart of course from those containing no tobacco.

Eventually we wanted to do more than drift horizontally on the sea's surface, and joined the Nairobi branch of the British Sub-aqua Club. BSAC training is considerably more comprehensive than the ubiquitous PADI (Professional Association of Diving Instructors) courses designed to get holiday makers diving in the shortest possible time and to provide a steady stream of income for the instructors. I am not criticising: PADI courses have introduced millions to the delights of SCUBA diving, but BSAC appealed to my inner scientist, covering as it does the changes which take place in the blood when it is not getting the usual mixture of nitrogen and oxygen, as well as the physiological effects of the substantial increases in pressure on the body underwater.

BSAC operates as a club, with experienced members instructing the novices and supervising the strict tests which all have to pass before they can move on to the next stage. We each bought our own equipment, including air cylinders and regulators, either from members who were leaving or when we were on home leave. The modern BCD, buoyancy control device, had not been developed and for flotation we wore time-expired life jackets which were given to us by East African Airways, only inflated when we returned to the surface.

We met on a weekday evening at a hotel near Westlands where we did exercises in the pool and, when we were ready, made some open water dives in Lake Naivasha, where the crater lake goes down to twenty metres or so. After gaining experience and confidence in the calm waters of the lake we had our first dive when staying at Diani, in the shallow waters round the reef. We ventured no deeper than ten metres but the excitement of rounding a bend in a coral canyon and coming face-to-face with a large grouper was enough to get me hooked on the endless beauty below the ocean's deceptively empty surface.

My second sea dive was in fairly shallow water just outside the reef north of Mombasa. I descended and allowed the fairly strong current to take me, drifting a few feet above the sea bed, lost in the magical sensation of flying through this wonderfully alien world, until my air ran low and I returned to the surface to find that, of course, our boat was almost lost in the distance. My inner scientist must have been off duty and had not alerted me to the blindingly obvious, that a metre covered on the sea bed is also a metre on the surface. Fortunately my old EAA life jacket still held the air which I puffed into the little tube as demonstrated so charmingly by the air stewardesses and, well-supported, I bobbed happily in the warm surface waters until the dive boat came and found me.

I have since dived in many places, from the Caribbean in the west to Borneo and the Philippines in the east; the magic never palls but the most abiding memories are of those early and ill-equipped dives on the Kenya coast.

One of our last visits to the coast was a quarterly area meeting of Round Table at Two Fishes Hotel at Diani. Bente drove down on the Friday morning with the wife of a friend; he and I followed after work, arriving about ten at night. We had two wonderful days relaxing from the stresses of work life, a couple of token meetings to discuss fund-raising and social activities, snorkelling over the reef, drinking beer by the lovely pool which snaked its way through the bar out to a terrace among the palms and dancing late into the night with friends. The nights were warm, the friendships were real: is it any wonder we so enjoyed our life in Africa?

8. THE MIDDLE YEARS

JEFF FULMER, MY NEW EMPLOYER at Skyline Advertising was a large man in every way, six foot four and weighing between 15 and 20 stone depending on how fit he was at any given time. He could put on many pounds in a couple of months then go on a low-carbohydrate diet and lose them again in weeks, he could chain-smoke for months and then stop abruptly and not appear to notice, drink enough to render most men legless then be teetotal for weeks. He had a towering personality, could dominate a room, could be a complete bully or could sit quietly as an observer.

He was born into a wealthy landowning family in Memphis, Tennessee, with a nanny whom he loved. When he was six, he was told he could no longer kiss her goodnight because she was black. He grew up with a very ambivalent attitude to women, to black people and most particularly to his parents and to rich white Americans. Jeff treated women in a nineteenth-century way, not crediting them in general with very much intelligence, but he was gallant, an antebellum throwback to his Southern roots.

He had been educated at Phillips Exeter Academy, one of the most exclusive of America's 'prep' – which we call public – schools. After a brief failed marriage, which produced a daughter from whom he was estranged, he joined the US Air Force and was posted to Turkey where, in addition to his military duties, he apparently had a brief affair with Eartha Kitt, one of my favourite singers. His father had built up a sizeable business manufacturing parts for the automobile industry, and his chosen heir was Jeff's older brother Arthur, the polar opposite to Jeff. They had both inherited their father's business instincts but Arthur was controlled, and not a man to show his emotions.

Jeff received an annual allowance of $50,000 mostly, I suspect, to keep him away from Memphis and prevent the possibility of him embarrassing the family. On leaving the Air Force he moved to Tangier, then a fairly wild freeport, where he fell in love with Frida Riddlesbarger, a beautiful Icelandic woman trapped with her daughter Lisa in an abusive and unhappy marriage. He also met Kurt and Ann Curtis, of whom more later. After a while he married Frida, drifted down to Nairobi, met Bill Purdy, who was looking for someone to take over the responsibility of Skyline Advertising, and acquired a majority share.

He lived life to excess with a careless disregard for his safety, both personal and financial. During one six-week period while we worked together, he wrote off a Mercedes, an Alpha Romeo and two Piper Cherokees. The first plane came to grief landing at the very rough airstrip at the Naivasha Marina Club, the nosewheel digging in to a warthog burrow; a couple of weeks later on a Sunday afternoon our phone rang: 'Hey Bill, I've done it again!' He'd flown up to Mount Kenya Safari Club with a friend for lunch and, when leaving, ignored conventional wisdom and tried to take off downhill rather than into the wind, with predictable consequences. I duly drove up to collect them, a round trip of some six hours. I decided never to let him fly me.

Jeff was also a man of high principles. Early on in my time at Skyline we were invited to pitch for the account of the local affiliate of British American Tobacco, one of the largest advertisers in East Africa. Although at times he was a heavy smoker, the health dangers of tobacco were beginning to be recognised and he refused to take on the account, deliberately passing up the opportunity to significantly enhance his business.

My work permit with Gill and Johnson was not transferable and, until a new permit specific to Skyline was issued, I was technically not permitted to work. The accounts department had recently installed one of the earliest small commercial computers, a Burroughs L2000, and I was the only person in the company capable of operating it. Without the invoices it produced cash flow would have ceased and the company would have rapidly ground to a halt, so I had to work. While waiting for my permit to be issued I did so at night, illegally, arriving at the office around six in the evening after the staff had left. I brought sandwiches to sustain me and drove home in the wonderful still of the night at around three in the morning.

The assistant accountant, Bruce Mitchell, was a middle-aged Englishman with no professional qualifications, reliable but slow and without the skills necessary to run the department, and certainly unable to handle Jeff's demands and mercurial temper. Bruce, married to a delightful Ugandan woman, apparently thought that he should have been promoted into my job; he complained to the Department of Immigration that he had not been offered it simply because he had an African wife and the permit was refused. When we realised what he had done, Jeff and I marched him the few hundred yards to the Immigration Department and pretty much forced him to confess that he was not up to the job. My work permit was duly issued and I could once more work during the day.

The creative atmosphere of an advertising agency was very unlike any environment I had ever experienced. Among other things, I was introduced to the pleasures of smoking marijuana, pot as it was then known. It had not been part of the culture when I was growing up. I had left London before the '60s really started to swing, and in Copenhagen my father-in-law was a senior police officer and using even such a mild drug would have been strictly frowned upon. In Nairobi, however, it was commonplace, readily and cheaply available. It was bought in the chicken market (I have never understood the connection between chickens and marijuana – another of life's small mysteries) where it was sold for 50 cents, a little under 30 pence in today's money, one rolled-up dried plant to each anonymous brown paper bag. Parties given by my Skyline colleagues were decidedly more interesting than soirées with fellow accountants – under the influence of pot Sly and the Family Stone is right up there with Mozart.

Jeff and I immediately got on well but it took a while for him to accept me as a junior partner rather than an employee, and initially I concentrated on running the accounts department as part of the management team. The company was reasonably successful, reflecting the growth in the economy, and although we were both occupied full time we began to discuss the opportunities opening up in tourism in this rapidly developing post-independent country. We decided to set up a separate company for this purpose, ambitiously named Capital Development International Ltd (CDIL), a name not of my choosing – I would have opted for something rather more understated. It was incorporated in the Cayman Islands – from the start we had ambitions to take its activities beyond East Africa – with an operating subsidiary in Kenya of which I was Managing Director.

Jeff decided to bring in his old friend Kurt Curtis from Tangier: when he arrived I instantly recognised a con man. Kurt was of medium height and portly, distinguished looking, very sharply dressed in a well-cut three-piece suit, with a neat but bushy grey beard, monocle and high heeled Texan boots. He would not have been out of place in an Agatha Christie mystery. His wife Ann was slim, beautiful and elegant, her jet-black hair always covered by a wide brimmed hat to protect her marble-white skin from the African sun – she could have been a character from the Addams Family. Ann usually had a small pet boa constrictor with her, a Freudian symbol perhaps of, as we soon found out, her nymphomania.

As his contribution to CDIL Kurt had brought with him the African rights to a supposedly highly effective treatment for arthritis, a noxious lotion which had to be applied wearing surgical gloves. The words 'snake oil' immediately came to my mind but, to my surprise, Jeff accepted it as another opportunity for profit. Of course, none of the product was ever sold. Jeff, strangely, was impressed by Kurt and of course I went along with it, while dropping quiet hints that I was unimpressed. Kurt always tried to dominate meetings and some people fell for his undoubted charm; several of my colleagues also succumbed to the charms of his wife.

As our ambitions were in the tourism industry and we had little to invest other than our enthusiasm, we thought it would be useful to develop a relationship with the Kenya Tourist Development Corporation (KTDC), who were empowered to make investments on behalf of the government. Their senior managers were fairly inexperienced, KTDC being less than ten years old and not much development having yet taken place, and we had to deal with some fragile egos. In our first serious meeting, at Jeff's suggestion Kurt took the lead, and I realised that his style was unlikely to work with inexperienced African civil servants. He dominated the meeting and the minutes he prepared from it referred to him making a 'succinct presentation'; from their reaction I realised that KTDC's managers shared my opinion of him. Even though Jeff remained supportive I began to look for an opportunity to have Kurt removed.

Fortunately he made that easy for me. He persuaded us that he had contacts in finance who might be interested in investing in Kenya's tourism, and he went on our behalf to London to meet them. On his return presented me with a wad of expense vouchers for reimbursement. I noticed that they included many bills from the same restaurant, sequentially numbered, obviously from a pad stolen from a waiter – you can take the boy out of auditing, but fortunately you can't take auditing out of the boy. I confronted him with this in the next of our regular Monday morning meetings: he became aggressive and bizarrely accused me of 'sophistry' but of course he had no defence. Exit Kurt.

The others in the management team of Skyline were not particularly happy with Jeff being distracted from the core business of the advertising agency, and after some negotiation the two companies were separated, with Jeff retaining a minority share in Skyline and he and I becoming the sole shareholders in CDIL, split two thirds/one third. We took on two employees, Jeff's very efficient secretary Gulzaar and a clerk, Eddy, and rented some first-floor offices in a charming old two-storey building dating back to the beginning of the century. The heart of the office was a large rectangular room and rather than clutter it with desks we built workstations, effectively desktops attached to the wall at various heights so we could work sitting or standing as the mood took us. This was where Jeff and I spent most of our time, throwing ideas around and making grandiose plans. Gulzaar had a separate office, the typewriters of the time being noisy, and there were a couple of meeting rooms and a small kitchen.

For years Jeff's family in Memphis had been friendly with Kemmons Wilson, the founder of Holiday Inns. Kemmons had been a building contractor with a large family and after a road trip in the early fifties, during which he was disappointed by the standards of available accommodation, he had decided there was a market for inexpensive family-friendly hotels. He built his first hotel in Memphis and it was an immediate success. That one hotel rapidly grew into the largest hotel chain in the world, and by the early 1970s there were more than 1,500 Holiday Inns, some owned, some franchised, with more than half a million rooms in total. There were, apparently, more people sleeping in a Holiday Inn bed each night than there were soldiers in the US army. Through contacts in Memphis, Jeff and I arranged to meet Kemmons in London. He had a busy schedule but found time to share an enjoyable breakfast with us at his hotel. He was interested in our plans for hotel developments in Africa and we made an informal agreement that, if we came up with a suitable project, Holiday Inns would grant us an exclusive franchise for East Africa.

Back in Kenya Jeff and I started making ambitious plans. I have happy memories of weekends spent driving round the country, looking for potential hotel sites. A couple of acres close to Nairobi's city centre, a bluff in the Taita Hills with a stunning view over Tsavo West, a beachfront plot of 50 acres or so, coral limestone with sandy inlets. I remember the warm companionship and shared dreams. I always drove and he was relaxed beside me, usually with an arm round my shoulders. We talked endlessly and we also drove in silence – there was an extraordinary rapport between us. We found an elephants' graveyard and we counted crocodiles in the Tana River; we stood together on the misty flanks of Mount Marsabit, where I saw my first ever greater kudu as we watched a camel train wend its way in from the northern deserts.

Eventually we bought the Nairobi plot, on which we planned to build our first hotel. The site had a moderate gradient and a fair bit of exposed rock. We commissioned a local architect, Chris Archer, to design a 200-room hotel, explaining that we wanted a building of character, using the contours of the land and incorporating where possible some of the exposed rocky surfaces. He came back a couple of weeks later with his initial sketches which were, predictably, the plot bulldozed flat and a tower block. I have since discovered that there is a tendency in architects to want to design prominent landmarks, monuments to their skills. We explained that we wanted a building to blend subtly into the landscape; a week later he came back with version two, a podium to effectively level out the attractively sloping plot and, unsurprisingly, a tower block on top.

The following weekend was Easter, which Jeff and I spent by the pool of the Muthaiga Club where, with graph paper, balsa wood, a Stanley knife and glue we built a scale model of what we wanted. I am not artistic and those who have been close to me over the years have been gently critical of my DIY skills, but I was quite proud of that model. It was a hollow rectangle, two storeys at the top end of the slope, four storeys at the bottom, with a central atrium which would feature some of the rocky outcrops. We presented the model to Chris who, a couple of weeks later, came back to us having had the brilliant idea of a rectangular block enclosing an atrium, et cetera et cetera; we pandered to his ego and admired his drawings which were, of course, exactly what we had wanted from the beginning.

We then set about the difficult bit, raising finance. Jeff had his regular dividend from the family business, $50,000 a year, but did not have access to capital; neither of course did I. The easy route would have been finance from a contractor but in the long run that is invariably expensive There are very many projects where undercapitalised entrepreneurs have relied on contractor finance, struggled to service the expensive loans, and had their creation repossessed by the contractor, refinanced far more cheaply and sold on. We made a half-hearted attempt to raise money from the local community but it attracted little interest – the age of inexpensive mass travel was on the horizon but its impact was not fully appreciated, oil prices were rising rapidly and there was a general nervousness about the way world's finances were going. There was tentative interest expressed by some of the community of Asian traders. I had a phone call from a young man who said his family, who owned a carpet store on Bazaar Street, would like to invest $100,000. I asked him if that would be equity or loan – we would have been happy with either. 'Oh no, sir,' he replied, 'cash.' That $100,000, at that time, is equivalent to well over half a million today, an indication of how successful some of the very understated Indian traders were.

A year or so after meeting Kemmons in London, I visited the United States for the first time to finalise the details of our collaboration. I flew to Boston's Logan Airport, where I was collected by Jeff's old school friend from Phillips Exeter, Bob Ory. I had met Bob a few months earlier when he visited Nairobi, and he, his wife and their three teenage boys all came to meet me, and drove me the 50 miles to their house in Worcester, Massachusetts.

To them I must have been exotic, a white man from Africa with the strange ways that Americans expect of foreigners. Although they themselves did not drink, Bob knew that I enjoyed a beer and had bought a six pack of Coors specially for me. When we sat down for supper – I can't call it dinner and have never got used to the American pattern of eating, with the evening meal usually served about six o'clock and accompanied by coffee – they put a plate of food and the six pack in front of me. The concept of drinking alcohol with a meal was foreign to them, and as I poured myself a beer and drank they stared, fascinated, as if they expected to see horns sprout from my forehead. They were of course wonderfully hospitable hosts, but for all Bob's expensive education he was still very much a small-town American. We spent a couple of days together in New York, staying at a Holiday Inn in the Upper West Side, and he would not allow us to venture out after dark, claiming that the streets were unsafe.

From New York I flew on down to Memphis and took a taxi from the airport to the Holiday Inn in Holiday City, the beating heart of the enormous hospitality empire. It was early evening and as the taxi drew up at the hotel I saw my name in lights, for the first, and I have to confess only, time: there on the traditional Holiday Inn Great Sign I saw 'Holiday City welcomes Bill Samuel from Nairobi'.

I walked up to the reception desk: 'You have a reservation for me, I believe. I'm Bill Samuel from Nairobi.'

She scanned the register, at that time a traditional bound book, ran her finger down the column of names and looked up slightly puzzled. 'We have no booking under that name, sir.'

That was the first time I realised that the air of efficiency that America tries to give out does not always match the reality. Fortunately a room was available.

Having settled into my room I called one of the contacts Jeff had given me, his cousin Danny Copp, who was about my age. 'Hey Bill, I've been expecting to hear from you. Look, can I call you back in a few minutes?' I assumed he was busy but when he called back a short time later he said 'Okay Bill, tomorrow you're coming to us for supper, Friday Arthur and Nancy have organised a small party for you, Saturday you're having dinner with Jeff's parents and Herb and Nell Levy are expecting you on Sunday evening.' My social programme for the next few days was organised in minutes, my first experience of the wonderful American hospitality. American efficiency may be exaggerated; its reputation for hospitality and generosity are not.

Jeff's family were old money. His parents lived about a mile from downtown Memphis, keeping their beloved horses on the last 30 acres of what had once been the family plantations. They were in their mid-eighties, and dinner was served by their butler Andrew, in full uniform including tail coat and white gloves. For all their wealth they didn't travel much and were fascinated by what they called my British accent. They produced a book of the speeches of Winston Churchill, one of their heroes, and persuaded me to read from it. Mimicry is not one of my talents but I did my best and they were happy.

At some point during the evening Mrs. Fulmer referred to attitudes changing after the war, a comment which didn't quite fit into the context of our conversation. I asked to which war she was referring, assuming it would be either of the World Wars of the 20th century. 'Why, the War of Northern Aggression', she replied.

It was a Saturday evening and the conversation got round to church, very much part of their life. They were of course Episcopalian, the American equivalent of the Church of England which had figured in my childhood. I asked out of interest whether Andrew went to the same church; they looked at me, puzzled.

'Well, of course not, he's a niggrah.'

In the 1970s segregation in the States was alive and well. It didn't only apply to African-Americans. Herb and Nell Levy, wealthy friends of Jeff, had sold their New York-based business a couple of years earlier and retired to Memphis, where they found that they couldn't join the golf club because they were Jewish.

On my first morning in Memphis I walked the short distance from the hotel to the corporate headquarters for a meeting with William Lea, the newly appointed Holiday Inns' representative for Africa. I was in the elevator when the doors opened and Kemmons got in with a couple of his colleagues. He looked at me for a brief moment then recognition dawned: 'Well, hi Bill, what are you-all doing in Memphis?' Our London breakfast had been almost a year before – he had an impressive memory.

William and I agreed the rough outline of an informal franchise arrangement under the terms of which CDIL had exclusive rights to develop Holiday Inns in Africa. I persuaded them to throw in Saudi Arabia and the Arabian Gulf, which they did without question. It was only a couple of years since Saudi had taken control of its own oil production and started to flex its financial muscles; the region did not figure in the strategic planning of most of America's business community.

The following weekend, before returning to Nairobi, I flew to Philadelphia to stay with my old school friend Howard Pierce. He kept a sailing boat on the Chesapeake Bay and early on the Saturday morning, together with his wife Gillian and their two boys, we drove down to the little marina where it was moored. As soon as we crossed the state line into Maryland we stopped at a liquor store to pick up a flagon of gin and a flagon of whisky, setting the pattern for the weekend.

It was a couple of days of warm reminiscence, going back to childhood. We had first met as twelve year olds nervously sitting our scholarship exams at Harrow; we had sailed together on the Norfolk Broads, and I had stayed with Howard a couple of times at the lovely Trearddur Bay Hotel on Anglesey, of which his father was the manager. We set sail about nine o'clock and Howard immediately poured us each a large gin and tonic. The weather was perfect, warm sunshine and a fair breeze, and we had a wonderful day's sailing before rafting up in the middle of the bay with a dozen other yachts and socialising late into the night.

The boys were ten and eight, I was mellow with alcohol, and told them stories of life in Africa. Howard came to stay with me in London some thirty years later and told me that his sons, now grown men with families of their own, still refer to me as African Bill. Since then I have kept in contact and visited Howard as his successful career in electrical engineering took him round the world, visiting him at various times in Florida, Zurich and Beijing.

Back in Kenya we continued to develop our plans. Jeff had some friends, Charles and Jean Hayes, who owned a small tourist lodge on the shore of lake Naivasha. Jean was an actress who had come to Kenya in the early 1950s to join the Donovan Maule Theatre Company. Her journey out to Nairobi had been adventurous. She flew with a fellow actor and amateur pilot in an old seaplane which crashed attempting to land on the upper Nile in Egypt. They were forced to continue by the BOAC London – Cape Town flying boat service, which landed at Lake Naivasha, the closest stretch of open water to Nairobi. The landing stage was on Crescent Island, the beautiful partial rim of an old volcano which was home to some 400 species of birds. Jean fell instantly in love, with the abundance of birds and with the island, and promised herself that one day she would buy it.

Her husband Charles was a journalist, originally with the *News Chronicle* in London, who moved to Nairobi at about the same time. Charles got occasional parts at the Donovan Maule, where they met and fell in love, eventually marrying. Charles set up *Taifa*, a Swahili newspaper which, after a couple of years, he sold to the Aga Khan's media company, becoming editor of its Daily Nation. By the time I met them Jean had fulfilled her dream of buying Crescent Island, had become a recognised expert in the recording of birdsong and was running Andrew Crawford Productions, a sound recording studio in Nairobi of which Skyline Advertising was a major customer

Charles, in one of the rare affluent periods of his life, had bought Sanctuary Farm on the lake shore opposite Crescent Island. He and Jean pooled their resources and set up the Naivasha Marina Club, building a restaurant and bar on a low bluff looking out over the crater lake cradled by the half-moon of Crescent Island. Behind that they built a circle of a dozen or so rondavels around an unfiltered concrete swimming pool. Hot water came from the old oil drums set in nooks at the back of each one; one of the staff would go round in the early morning building a log fire under them. It was simple, effective and cheap.

Jean was busy running the recording studio in Nairobi while Charles attempted to manage the club, but he was not commercially minded and lacked any relevant experience. The club was losing money, and they invited Jeff and me to invest, so for the paltry sum of £3,000 we became one-third shareholders, our first actual investment in the hospitality industry.

We operated very much on a shoestring. Charles had no money to invest, Jean was unprepared to throw good money after bad and Jeff and I needed to conserve our resources for our proposed Holiday Inn development, so we improvised. I recall one Friday, when we expected a few weekend visitors but the bar stocks had been severely depleted, maxing out my credit card at a Nairobi liquor store in order to replenish them. At one point the chef quit and the delightful clerk who worked in our Nairobi office volunteered to do the cooking. Eddie Sirengo's signature dish was steak Diane but, as we soon discovered, the rest of his repertoire was decidedly limited. The kitchen adjacent to the restaurant had a rudimentary corrugated iron roof which leaked copiously; it is hard to cook a perfect steak Diane with rainwater dripping into the pan.

Although our part ownership of the club caused us a degree of stress, it also gave us enormous enjoyment. For a couple of years we would go up as a family most weekends; Bente and I would dabble in housekeeping, food preparation, swimming pool maintenance and anything else that needed doing while Marina and Margaret passed the time swimming in the pool or the lake, exploring or reading. One of the photos I treasure most from that time is of the two of them swimming in the lake with Jeff's ten-year-old son Johnnie, their blond hair in beautiful contrast to the pink water lilies around them.

The effort we put in was more than compensated for by the sublime pleasure of sitting on the veranda outside the bar at sundown looking out across the lake, the fringes of which were dotted with dead Acacia trees, skeletal perches for fish eagles and pelicans competing for the bounty of the warm tropical water. The large group of resident hippos would be splashing in the shallows beneath us, the soundtrack the cry of the fish eagle and the chirp of the cicada. After a few beers we would enjoy one of Eddie's steaks and sleep the sleep of the exhausted in one of the simple, rough-built rondavels.

The island was home to a fluctuating population of wild animals, which came and went as the water level allowed access from the mainland. There were always antelope and a small herd of buffalo, but our favourites were Rosemary, a handsome ostrich, and Twiggy, a young giraffe. Rosemary was unusually unafraid of humans, had great curiosity and like a magpie was attracted by shiny things. If she saw a visitor with a camera she would set off in pursuit, and we saw many a tourist looking nervously over their shoulders and wondering whether or not it would be wise to run as Rosemary trotted after them. Twiggy, about eight foot tall, loved to have her chest scratched; she would signal that she had had enough by suddenly dropping her head like a pile-driver and if the scratcher didn't move fast enough they came away with a nasty headache.

During the period of our ownership the film *Living Free*, the sequel to *Born Free* which chronicled Joy Adamson's life working with lions, was filmed on Crescent Island. The island varied in size from 800 to 2,000 acres depending on the seasonal fluctuations of the lake's water level. When the water was low we reached the island by wading along a short causeway, taking care to remove the leeches which always attached themselves to our feet, at other times by boat from the club. We visited several times during the filming and my young daughters were allowed to play with the lion cubs, the real stars of the film. When the cubs first arrived they were six-week-old bundles of fur with the exuberance and playfulness of all kittens; by the time filming finished they were six months old and considerably larger. They would signify the end of playtime with a good-natured swipe of a hefty paw, and after we had been given a few bloody tramlines down our arms we reluctantly gave up playing with them.

A few years ago I re-visited Lake Naivasha, now the heart of a huge cut-flower industry employing many thousands of people. Through the depredations of this industry the water level has fallen at least 10 feet, Crescent Island is no longer an island and the little Naivasha Marina Club where we had spent so many idyllic weekends is now an abandoned ruin, marooned a hundred yards from the new lake shore. Joy was murdered a few years after the film was made, as in his turn was her delightful husband George – Joy by a disgruntled employee, George by poachers. *Sic transit*, and all that.

In the meantime, to generate income for the company, and of course to find out a little about how hotels work, we tendered for and won a contract for the renovation of the Grand Hotel in Khartoum, Sudan. We retained the services of an experienced hotelier, Norman Jarman, who had been instrumental in building up African Tours and Hotels (AT & H), a small chain of hotels and tourist lodges, and he and I flew up to Khartoum. I finalised the agreement with the Sudan Tourism Authority (STA), the government body that owned the hotel, while Norman did the technical appraisal.

The Grand Hotel was an imposing but very run-down relic of the colonial era when Sudan had been administered by the British, and the budget only allowed for modest and largely cosmetic improvements. However, I got on well with the management of the STA and told them of our relationship with Holiday Inns. They were immediately interested, as Khartoum lacked modern hotels, and showed me a beautiful two-acre site on the south bank of the Blue Nile, just before the junction of the two arms of that magnificent river. Before I left, we had drawn up a memorandum of understanding for CDIL to develop a Holiday Inn on the site.

I much enjoyed my week in Khartoum. Although we got on well, Norman and I had little in common and I went for long walks alone in the evening beside the river. Shortly after we moved to Nairobi I had read Alan Moorhead's *The White Nile* and *The Blue Nile*, wonderfully descriptive books about early African exploration. The White Nile begins its 4,000 mile journey north to the Mediterranean at Jinja in Uganda, flowing out of Lake Victoria and tumbling over some fairly spectacular waterfalls and rapids before it reaches Sudan. Here it slows down and spreads out into the vast wetlands of the Sudd, its myriad channels meandering through floating islands of papyrus and bulrushes, then makes its leisurely way on to Khartoum. The Blue Nile is a very different river, rising in the highlands of Western Ethiopia and cascading through dramatic gorges until it reaches Khartoum, falling twice as far in less than half the distance.

Where these two very different rivers meet in Khartoum there is a distinct demarcation, the silt-laden waters of the White Nile and the clear mountain waters of the Blue running side-by-side. It is a good few miles downstream before these waters begin to merge as they run on towards the biblical lands of Upper Egypt, eventually entering the Mediterranean through the wide delta at Alexandria well over 1,000 miles to the north. I had never expected to stand at the junction of these two magnificent rivers: now we potentially had a hotel site quarter of a mile upstream.

AT & H had a dozen or so hotels dotted around Kenya, mostly small but including the gems of Kilaguni in Tsavo West National Park and Mountain Lodge on the southern slopes of Mount Kenya. The market capitalisation of the company was not much over a hundred thousand pounds, as it had a fair amount of debt, and it occurred to us that if we acquired it we would have an excellent springboard for the development of a chain of Holiday Inns. Its management were, understandably, unwilling to support any attempt for outsiders to get control of the company, particularly outsiders like Jeff and me who were not part of the old Nairobi establishment. But it was very tempting, for such a very modest sum, to acquire not only a dozen operating hotels but also a tour business with a fleet of vehicles so We made an offer to the 200 or so shareholders. They closed ranks and eventually, with less than 10% acceptances, we gave up. We had made the offer fairly tongue-in-cheek: it was a bit of fun and light relief compared to the grown-up stuff of putting together a proper hotel development, and I can at least say that I once made a hostile bid for a public company.

Meanwhile, the grown-up stuff continued. William Lea flew out to Kenya to assess the potential for a chain of Holiday Inns in East Africa. We met him at the airport and he showed all the uptight insecurity of a small-town American travelling for the first time. He was only due to stay for a few days so we took him on a whistle-stop tour designed to impress him with the great variety which Kenya had to offer, driving him directly from the airport to Kilaguni Lodge in Tsavo West Game Park, which was and remains one of my favourites.

After an early dinner, during which the sun set with the

rapidity only found near the equator, we were sitting on the veranda looking out over the floodlit water hole. Africa, as it sometimes can, put on an impressive pageant just for us. There were plains game everywhere: giraffes, zebras, a few buffalo and a little family of warthog running around with their tails erect; there were elephants browsing in the clump of acacias off to the left, and a lion came down to the water to drink. After no more than fifteen minutes of this spectacle, which would have had most watchers entranced, William announced in a bored voice that he was off to bed. As I look back I know he was jetlagged, having just flown from Memphis to Nairobi with a brief stopover in London, but at the time I thought it offensive and crass. I was showing him the Africa that I loved and he was decidedly unimpressed.

The following day we drove down to the coast to stay at a lovely beach house opposite Chale Island south of Mombasa, owned by our architect Chris Archer. We had an excellent dinner of local seafood beautifully prepared by Chris's cook and retired for an early night. I was sharing a large room with William and when I was in the bathroom I saw a small scorpion in the shower tray. Before going back to bed I leant over William, who was on the verge of sleep, and whispered in his ear 'There's a scorpion in the bathroom.' He got very little sleep that night.

It was a petty and childish thing to do but childishly I thought I had in some way got revenge for his behaviour the previous evening. A few months later he moved from Memphis to Nairobi and of course we became good friends; he was a very supportive ally in our hotel project.

A couple of months later we persuaded Kemmons to visit Kenya so he could see for himself the potential for tourism in that strikingly beautiful, stable black African country. Through our friend Dawson Mlamba, Permanent Secretary in the Ministry of Foreign Affairs, we arranged for him to meet the President, Jomo Kenyatta. We were fairly certain that they would get on. They both had great achievements behind them and although

Kemmons was fifteen years younger he had, like Mzee – 'old man', as the President was affectionately and respectfully known – begun to hand over the reins of power.

We were told by the usual sycophantic courtiers that to impress the President we would have to make a substantial donation to his family charities, which we were not prepared to do. I had found out early in my relationship with Jeff that, for all the wildness of his youth, he had a very strong moral character and sense of right and wrong. We did, however, buy a small gift for the President, a stone ashtray which cost the princely sum of seventy pounds, with which Jomo was delighted. Those surrounding him, corrupt themselves, assumed he was also corrupt: he was not.

We were also told that Kemmons was most unlikely to get more than half an hour of Jomo's time. As it turned out, they spent a leisurely two hours chatting at the President's farm outside Nairobi, two old men reminiscing about the completely different paths they had taken through life.

Over dinner that evening we talked to Kemmons about the renovation of the Grand Hotel in Khartoum, and the possibility of developing a Holiday Inn on the Nile. His question, 'What's it like, dealing with Ayrabs?', suggested that, despite being chairman of the largest hotel company in the world, he had little knowledge of anything outside Europe and North America.

Eventually we reached an agreement with KTDC and Holiday Inns to each put up one-third of the equity of £1 million, with CDIL putting in the land and all the work done so far for the final third. Meetings were set up involving Kenyan civil servants and large white American men from Memphis Tennessee. These meetings would go on for several days, as African meetings can, but sooner or later one of the Americans would lose his patience and come out with something along the lines of 'Cain't you niggrahs get anything right?', not a winning line in black Africa, and the meeting would fall apart, taking another six months to re-convene.

It was of course essential that we continued as if the development was a certainty. In addition to the equity, we needed $2 million of loan finance, much of which would be to fit out and equip the building. As most of the equipment to be imported would come from the United States, we approached the Overseas Private Investment Company (OPIC), a US-government-owned institution set up to finance US exports.

I made a second visit to the States to discuss details of the project with Holiday Inns, and to finalise the loan finance from OPIC. I stayed in Memphis with the likeable and gregarious marketing vice-president George Falls, whom I had got to know on my previous trip. George was away travelling the evening I arrived and had left a key for me with his neighbours. The house was a little set back from the road and, when they led me in through the small yard, I noticed that the remains of the party he had had the night before hadn't been cleared away – George was a sociable bachelor who enjoyed entertaining and had left very early in the morning. I suggested I at least clear away the bottles of liquor still standing on the trestle table and the case of beer underneath it in case they were stolen during the night. The neighbours were amused. 'No one's gonna steal from ol' George,' they told me. I suspect that downtown Memphis has changed in the fifty years since.

George returned late that evening and the following morning we walked together the few yards to his favourite diner for breakfast. It was the scene from so many classic movies: all the regulars knew each other, class, background and colour were irrelevant and the conversation, ranging from sport to politics, flowed easily. George was the well-educated white vice-president of a major multinational company, his regular breakfast companions were mostly black, cleaners, postmen and office workers – it would not happen in the UK.

During this trip, William arranged for me to visit a hotel being built in Huntington, West Virginia using a new and innovative construction method. My host, the developer, was also the mayor of Huntington. He liked to live up to his image of a West Virginia lawmaker, wearing a Stetson, cowboy boots and twin pearl-handled revolvers while driving a large white Cadillac convertible. As he was a short, bald and overweight businessman he struggled to project the image he sought. Forty years later, in one of life's frequent small coincidences, one of the guests at a supper party given by our neighbours in Northamptonshire told me she came from Huntington. I mentioned having met the mayor, and described him. She smiled and said, 'That would be Mayor Frankel. I used to date his son.'

On one of my free evenings I had dinner alone in a restaurant beside the wide, slow, muddy Mississippi, watching the parade of paddle steamers, with their complement of tourists no doubt imagining themselves in some romanticised version of the nineteenth century. The background music in the restaurant included *Killing Me Softly* by Roberta Flack, which I had first heard a few days before. It rapidly became, and remains, one of my favourite pieces of music. I was thousands of miles from home and my little family, enjoying experiences which they would not share, and I realised that my wife and I were almost imperceptibly beginning to drift apart. At the time it was inconceivable to me that we would ever separate, but looking back I realise that that evening of contemplation, with its background of music that was mine rather than ours, was the start of an inexorable process of separation which was to last more than twenty years.

My final day in Memphis was a Saturday, and Kemmons invited me to a small barbecue party at his fairly modest home. Afterwards William drove me to the airport in his large white convertible – the South likes its white convertibles – steering with one hand and holding a large martini in the other – drink-driving regulations in Tennessee at the time were fairly relaxed.

I flew to Washington to finalise the draft finance agreement which OPIC had drawn up. That Monday was 30 June, a significant date, as I was to find out. I arrived at the impressive offices of OPIC, right in the heart of Washington, DC, feeling very much like someone from out-of-town there on false pretences, which in a way I was – our corporate financial structure had been created with an element of smoke and mirrors. However, I was greeted warmly, introduced to the team who had prepared the loan agreement and taken to a meeting room where we spent several hours working through the details.

At midday they brought me a typical gargantuan American sandwich and a pot of insipid coffee, and left me to check and agree the amended draft. I spent a couple of hours going through the fine print and, as the afternoon wore on, I sensed a degree of nervousness; one or other of the negotiators would look in every half hour or so to check that I was OK, had enough coffee and ask if I had any questions. This really surprised me as I thought the nervousness had been entirely on my side. It was, after all, the first time I had tried to borrow two million dollars.

When I was finally happy with the agreement, towards the end of the day, I signed and they signed and we went off for a drink to celebrate. They then explained to me that it was the last day of their financial year and that the following year's allocation of funds depended on commitments made during this year. Had we realised that we would have probably asked for more.

With the full three million needed for the project provisionally committed, we arranged a grand ground-breaking ceremony for which Mike Rose, a senior vice president of Holiday Inns who was to go on to become its CEO, flew out. He and Richard Maina, the head of the Kenya Tourist Development Corporation, each dug out a token spade-full of earth, but we did not start any serious construction work, very aware that, as they say, there's many a slip. And of course, slips there were.

Having spare time and entrepreneurial leanings we also looked at other business ventures. Electronic calculators had just come on the market and seemed brilliant. We imported 200 from Hong Kong at a landed cost of more than £100 each, and took on a young student to sell them to offices in Nairobi.

Calculators were one of the few things in the mid-1970s to fall in price with extraordinary rapidity and after we had sold a couple of dozen, mostly at a loss, we realised our future did not lie in consumer electronics.

Jeff was very taken by the American idea of summer camps for teenagers and decided there would be a market in the US for something similar to be done in Kenya. He had a friend, a Major Hugh, whose surname I forget, who was a retired English army officer complete with trilby hat and tweed jacket and could have been transplanted from a minor racecourse in the UK. Hugh was prepared to be tour leader, and we planned an itinerary which included visits to various game parks and a stay at the Marina Club. We negotiated group rates for flights from New York with East African Airways, placed enticing ads in *National Geographic* and waited for the applications to flood in. What we got was a tiny trickle: Jeff's assumption that his fellow Americans shared his appetite for exotic adventures proved wrong. Eventually five rather spoilt young Americans had a fantastic safari and we lost money.

The Danish engineer who had replaced Hans Eric told me that the land where the cement company quarried its gypsum also had huge deposits of bentonite, a clay used extensively in oil drilling, an activity which was seeing extraordinary growth in the Arabian Gulf. The major source of the material was Benton, Ohio, more than 500 miles from New York, itself many thousands of miles sailing from the Gulf, which is pretty much on Kenya's doorstep. We sensed an opportunity, and asked East African Railways to quote for shipment by the train-load, which proved to be an unfamiliar concept to them – we couldn't shift them from their initial price per kilogram even though we were hoping to ship hundreds of tons. Undeterred, we sent samples to the UK for analysis, only to be told that the silica content was unacceptably high.

This unbroken history of failure persuaded us to stick to tourism development, where new opportunities continued to present themselves while the proposed Nairobi Holiday Inn experienced its delays and setbacks.

We decided to pursue other potential developments. We were approached by the owner of a beachfront hotel in Watamu, who was interested in affiliating with Holiday Inns. I arranged to have dinner with him one Saturday evening and borrowed Jeff's beautiful Alfa Romeo 2000 Spyder for the drive down from Nairobi. Being a Saturday, the traffic was not particularly heavy and it was a glorious drive. I had the roof down, the wind in my hair and clocked 125 mph on the long straight stretch from Tsavo to Voi. I covered the 300 plus miles from Nairobi to Mombasa in a little under four hours, a journey which usually took six. Nothing came of the meeting but I had had a memorable drive, my heart singing with the beauty of the country – wonderful.

Dawson Mlamba arranged for us to visit the Finance Minister in Zanzibar to discuss the potential for a Holiday Inn – he also had responsibility for tourism. Zanzibar has its own unique character. It is a beautiful tropical island peopled by Africans whose culture has more in common with Oman, two thousand miles to the north, than the mainland a few miles to the west – the legacy of the many centuries of Arab influence. For more than 150 years, until 1963, the island was the dominant half of the Sultanate of Zanzibar and Oman. To walk through the capital Stone Town is almost to be in Muscat.

On a sultry evening heavy with the perfume of spices I wandered through the town and quietly watched old men sitting on the pavement playing chess. I passed the old Sultan's Palace and saw, in a corner of its courtyard, a great pile of copper cooking pots, each one, I irreverently thought, large enough to boil a missionary, and Africa once again lived up to my childhood dreams. More prosaically, when we visited the Finance Minister in his lovely old office looking out over the sea, I asked him what the country did with the substantial reserves it had accumulated from the strong demand for its main export, cloves. 'They're in there', he replied, pointing to the large old safe sitting against the wall behind him.

We were taken on a drive across the middle of the island, through spice plantations, to the east coast, which at the time was almost uninhabited, ours the only footprints on the glorious white sand beaches. Part of me saw this was crying out for development; a larger part asked 'Why?' I have since been back a couple of times: developed, it has lost much of its magic.

Further afield a contact working in Saudi Arabia put us in touch with a wealthy Saudi family who were interested in developing a hotel in Riyadh. Saudi Arabia by then was awash with the cash flowing in from oil – the price of which had risen dramatically in the early 1970s following their taking control of its production – but it was desperately short of hotel rooms to cater for the huge increase in the number of commercial visitors. There were, at the time, only three hotels of a standard acceptable to international visitors in the whole of Riyadh, a total of some 600 rooms, all of them running at over 100 per cent occupancy as visitors queued for rooms to become available.

The family to whom we were introduced were the sons of the physician to King Saud, the first king of Saudi Arabia, who had generously gifted their father 5,000 acres of desert land just outside the Riyadh metropolitan area. At the time it had little commercial value but now, as Riyadh has expanded from the seven hundred thousand occupants at the time of my first visit to a city of seven million plus, worth many billions.

Jeff and I arranged to visit and, as Saudi Arabia did not have any representation in East Africa, we had to travel via Beirut to collect our visas. I knew very little about Lebanon, and the first major surprise was the food – supper on the first night was an eye-opening and life-enhancing treat. It was my introduction to the delights of Lebanese cuisine, with its humous, tabbouleh, baba ghanoush and so much more, and I have enjoyed it ever since. The next surprise was the beauty of the landscape and of the climate. It was early February, the temperature was a springlike 20° and the backdrop snow-covered mountains with some quite acceptable skiing.

We rented a car and drove along the Bekaa Valley, intending to cross back over the mountains down to the coast well north of the city, but snowdrifts made the roads impassable. The valley itself was beautiful, lush and fertile, with villages which seem to alternate between French-influenced Christian with small pavement cafés serving French food and wine, and Arabic, where the cafés specialised more in aromatic coffee and hookahs.

At that stage of my career I was beginning to think of life after Nairobi and, as our business appeared to be moving in the right direction and that direction was generally north-east, I thought that Beirut would be a wonderful place to live for a few years. Sadly, a few months later, civil war broke out and the country descended into the chaos from which it has never fully recovered.

After collecting our visas on the Monday morning we boarded the flight for Riyadh. We had stocked up with alcohol at the Nairobi duty-free, as we were aware that we would not be able to buy it in Saudi. I had a bottle of whisky carefully buried among my clothes in my suitcase, Jeff a bottle of gin in his briefcase. Reading the in-flight magazine, we learned that even possession of alcohol was a serious crime in Saudi. This is now widely known, but at that time Saudi Arabia was a mystery. Jeff discreetly secreted his bottle down the front of his pants – he was, as I have said, a very large man. We both sweated as we went through customs but fortunately our illicit alcohol was not detected.

We were collected by our host and taken to his guest villa in the suburbs of Riyadh, where we met up with the friend who had introduced us and his colleague, both British businessmen attempting to make a living through trading on their contacts. The following morning our host took us by taxi to his offices in Riyadh, the taxi driver charging him three rials. A few days later I made the same journey on my own, and the taxi driver asked for twenty rials; I told him that it should only cost three to which he replied, 'Okay, three.' The fine art of negotiation was not at the time well-developed in Saudi.

The site which the family proposed to develop was very central and ideal for a five-star international hotel, and we put up a proposal under which they would contribute the land and guarantee the loan finance, we would manage the project and run it for a number of years as a Holiday Inn franchise before handing it over to them. They were happy with the principle but haggled endlessly about the detail, all the time showing enthusiasm and discussing the enormous potential to replicate the idea throughout the Arabian Peninsula. To put this into chronological context, the UAE had only come into existence a couple of years before. Dubai was little more than a village on a creek, and neither it nor Abu Dhabi had a single international-standard hotel.

Jeff returned to Nairobi, leaving me to haggle and sort out the detail. The days went past with meeting after meeting, always in the evenings and my first experience of the Arab work pattern. We were taken to see the camel racing, a very sedate affair with no betting and of course no bars, very different to any racing I'd been to elsewhere. Our host's grandsons took us on a trip to see the land owned by their grandfather, a fourteen year old driving the large Cadillac. In the middle of the scrubby and arid desert we were shown a cave at the foot of a low escarpment where a few metres in there was a fast flowing and crystal-clear river, which apparently flowed underground all the way to the Arabian Gulf in the east. They told us that it was geologists tracing this river's course in the 1930s who first noticed the rock formations suggesting oil.

After a couple of weeks of such distractions I decided that we were not making any serious progress, and reluctantly called an end to the negotiations. I have since had considerable experience of negotiation in the Arab world and, had I known then what I know now, I believe that with a little bit more patience on my part we would have reached an agreement that could have led to a very profitable business. One of life's many 'what ifs?'.

It had been a time of dreams and ambitions and hopes, one of the happiest periods of my life, but flaws were developing. Back in Nairobi, relations with KTDC were becoming increasingly fractious, and Jeff's growing impatience with the endless meetings and sudden setbacks was becoming obvious. Little progress was made. Gradually our plans fell apart and, with them, our relationship.

Our quirky offices with the once-close team of Jeff, Gulzaar, Eddie and me became an unhappy place. Jeff and I took to working in separate rooms and I slowly detached myself. Having no private income, I started to take on other work.

Eventually something happened, some meeting turned sour, and I wrote Jeff a letter of which unfortunately I did not keep a copy, referring to the straw that broke this particular camel's back. I reluctantly severed our links, and moved on once again, this time to the construction industry. Jeff spent more and more time in the bar of the Muthaiga Club and the hotel never got built.

9. THE CHARACTERS

IN EVERY PART OF BOTH my professional and personal life in Kenya, I crossed paths with an extraordinary cast of characters, some of whom enriched our life there.

Karen Blixen's *Out of Africa* had given me a graphic insight into the lives of European settlers early in the twentieth century before we set foot in the country. While obviously much had changed since then, I discovered that those who remained still enjoyed a life of great privilege. Bob Wilson, one of the 'introductions' with which I arrived, was one of them.

Bob had made an enviable lifestyle for himself. He was the younger son of a farmer in the Scottish Borders and, as his brother was destined to take over the family farm, Bob had emigrated to Kenya in the early 1950s to try his hand at farming there. Within a decade he had built up a successful mixed farm on the Kinangop, the fertile plateau west of the Aberdare Mountains, part of what was then known as the White Highlands. Always innovative, he crossbred Santa Gertrudis cattle from the Kleberg family's King Ranch in Texas with Scottish Galloways, combining the former's resistance to arid conditions with the latter's high-quality beef to give a breed excellently suited to Kenya. As the country's independence approached, most of the large European-owned farms in the White Highlands were bought out under a UK-government-financed scheme and the land distributed to African farmers. Many of the European farmers left but those, like Bob, who were committed to the country opted to take Kenyan citizenship, a requirement for owning land in Kenya post-independence.

Bob used the proceeds from the compulsory purchase of his Kinangop farm to buy Embori Farm near Timau on the northern slopes of Mount Kenya. It was a dart-shaped 35,000 acres pointing at the towering twin peaks of Batian and Nelion, semi-arid cattle country no more than 1,000 metres above sea level in the north, with the equator cutting across its snow-covered southern tip at more than 4,000 metres.

Bob also had a comfortable flat a few hundred yards from the centre of Nairobi and a lovely house at Kilifi on the coast, where he indulged his passion for game fishing, moving between these three properties in a small plane or his battered old Mercedes. He contributed much to the successful development of agriculture in Kenya after the Second World War, and regularly won a handful of prizes at the Nairobi agricultural show.

In common with many farmers living in remote houses, Bob and his wife Marjorie were very hospitable and we visited them a couple of times, first on our own and later with Bente's parents. The house, which had been constructed by the previous owners, was a rambling stone bungalow nearly 3,000 meters above sea level, with large log fires in each room to counter the night-time chill. At the bottom of the farm, where the climate was hot and dry, Bob grew wheat and grazed cattle; at the top, where the equator crossed his land, there was snow and he kept sheep. In between these two extremes he experimented with many things: I recall that on our first visit he proudly showed us his one acre of garlic.

When he bought the land much of it was virgin forest and he had three Caterpillar bulldozers constantly clearing the trees to make way for his cattle and sheep. At the time we admired his enterprise in the interest of efficient agriculture; now of course it would rightly be seen as destroying something irreplaceable.

In addition to his farm labourers, Bob had a full complement of domestic staff and one of his house boys, from one of the hunter-gatherer tribes, would go into the forest from time to time and return with a selection of honey. I remember at breakfast being offered several from different parts of the forest, each with its own distinct flavour and deliciously natural. I also remember walking up to the top of the farm to find the sheep rooting around in snow as they would have done in his native Scotland. The line of the equator was marked there with cairns and, simply so I could say I had, I threw a snowball across it. Mount Kenya is one of only two places in the world where that is possible.

Through our membership of the Danish Society we made friends with Eric and Rita Larsen, long-time Kenya residents. Eric was an ex-Nazi, and during the war had been a colonel in the SS, the commanding officer of the Danish Viking Regiment. As a traitor to his country he was unable to return to Denmark, so lived out his life in exile. One evening at dinner at our house in Peponi Road he got drunk and became indiscrete. To the acute embarrassment of Rita, he shocked us by goose-stepping up and down our living room, proud of his SS affiliation. He told us that he had been a full colonel at the age of twenty-two and had led the capture of Kiev. 'For a short while I was the King of Kiev. I could have anything I wanted, women, wine, anything.'

Obviously heady stuff for a twenty-two year old, but we had the impression he had little remorse. I had recently read *The Odessa File* by Freddie Forsyth which I had assumed was a work of fiction until Eric showed us his Odessa membership card, and the false Swiss identity papers which Odessa provided to old SS members. Ironically, given his Nazi past, he was working for a company owned by Jack Block, member of one of Nairobi's most prominent Jewish families. Bente carried on seeing Rita but we never met socially again.

There was an active Nazi association in Nairobi which met

for lunch once a month in the Embassy Hotel where we had spent our first night in Africa. At one meeting in, I think, 1971, their guest speaker was Otto Skorzeny, the SS commander who had rescued Mussolini after Il Duce had been caught by the Allies. He had been invited to East Africa by the Uganda Asian community, who had wanted him to assassinate Idi Amin. He apparently considered it and went to Kampala to get the lie of the land but decided it would be too risky.

There were other villains who took advantage of the tolerance which had marked Kenya since its early colonial days. It was common knowledge that Jomo Kenyatta's personal assassin was an Englishman, Pat Shaw. An obese man widely suspected of being a paedophile, who ran an orphanage called the Starehe Boys Home, he was reputedly responsible for the deaths of several of the President's political enemies. He died in 2003, some say of a heart attack, and some say in a hail of bullets. Certainly at the time of his funeral the local press reported that bullets were fired at his coffin.

Nairobi, for all its apparent civilization, remained a pretty wild place. John Salter was a friend, fellow member of Round Table and managing director of Colgate Palmolive in East Africa He was known to be a good pistol shot and told us that he had been recruited as an unofficial bodyguard to the President. He attended formal dinners with instructions to carry a concealed gun and keep his eyes open. As it happens, he never had occasion to use it, but as he said he had no idea how many other 'unofficial bodyguards' there might be in the room, all armed, all nervous. John imagined the scenario if someone reached down to recover a lost napkin, one person pulled a gun and all the others followed suit: mayhem.

T Ras Makonnen, Guyana born but of Ethiopian descent, was an advisor to and close friend of Jomo Kenyatta. They had met in the UK in the 1930s, when Kenyatta was studying at the London School of Economics, and both were part of the tight-knit group of men, including Kwame Nkrumah, Marcus Garvey and Haile Selassie, who had campaigned for the independence of African and Caribbean countries. Makonnen had become a Kenyan citizen, and I had the great pleasure of meeting him a couple of times, once at a formal reception and later informally on a stand at the Nairobi Agricultural Show.

On our second meeting we chatted mainly about music. During his time in London Makonnen had met Paul Robeson, whom my mother also met – he had been a customer of Foyles music department. Makonnen had just returned from Lagos where, he told me, he had met, after a concert, a blind singer and jazz pianist.

'Was that Ray Charles', I asked, slightly awe-struck, Ray Charles being one of my musical heroes.

'Yes, Mr. Charles. That was his name.'

He was an understated and gentle man who in his younger days had been a political agitator and firebrand, like Kenyatta committed to the cause of African unity. Both were, I suspect, disappointed by the excessive pomp and circumstance which had become the major preoccupations of many independent African leaders.

While I was at Gill and Johnson, I had found the staff were as varied as the work. One of my colleagues had been a tall, beautiful white lady, Dot Raynes Simpson. I remember Dot at afternoon tea parties, elegantly dressed, always wearing a large-brimmed hat and long white gloves, usually accompanied by her beloved boxer dogs. I knew she had been awarded the OBE, but it was a while before I found out why. I had read *Something of Value* and *Uhuru*, novels by Robert Ruark, an American writing about Kenya in the 1950s, in one of which was an incident involving two European ladies whose farm in the foothills of the Aberdare mountains was attacked by the Mau Mau. The terrorists broke into the kitchen where the ladies were sitting, relaxing at the end of a long day. One of them unhesitatingly pulled out a revolver and with six bullets killed the five intruders. That was the beautiful, elegant and cultured Dot.

The longest-serving member of staff was an unambitious senior auditor who had joined the firm not long before the Second World War, at a time when some upcountry clients were only reachable on horseback. Over the years he had acquired a fund of stories and a fondness for alcohol. He lived alone in a small bungalow on a typically large plot in the suburb of Karen, named after Karen Blixen, who had lived there for twenty years on her coffee farm. One day he came into work and told us that the previous evening, after his usual intake of Tusker beer, he had heard an animal rummaging in the dustbins outside his kitchen door. He staggered drunkenly out, saw what he thought was a particularly large dog, kicked it hard on its backside and watched it slink off into the night. The following morning, sober, he went to inspect the damage and saw extremely large pawprints which were definitely feline rather than canine. I suspect not too many people could kick a wild lion in the bottom and survive to entertain their colleagues with the tale the next day.

One of the administrative staff, Mrs. Beverley, was a tall, angular and socially awkward middle-aged lady, either widowed or divorced – I never found out which. She had adopted at least a dozen African children, ranging in age from mid-teens down to toddlers, who lived with her in her large rambling house in one of the outer suburbs. I visited a few times and there was always a wonderful air of warmth and controlled chaos. One of the oldest girls, Elizabeth, had lost a leg through, I believe, bone cancer; that didn't stop her from climbing Mount Kenya, which is one of the physically toughest things I've ever done – the bravery and perseverance to do it on crutches is beyond my imagination. I last saw Elizabeth some years later when she was in the UK, studying art at Farnham Art College, swinging through my home town on her crutches.

We met many other powerful personalities during our

time there, some of whom, Joy and George Adamson, Armand and Michaela Denis, and Charles and Jean Hayes I have written of elsewhere. There were more entrepreneurs per head of population than I have come across anywhere else. Within my own circle of friends and acquaintances I think of Alan Doig, whose Bunson Travel at one time was the highest-performing sales outlet for BOAC; Pius Ngugi who, when I met him, was trying to raise finance to build a small pencil factory and is now one of the wealthiest men in Kenya; and Mansukh Shah, who ran a pharmacy in central Nairobi and also owned factories making sanitary towels and barbed wire. Years later Mansukh was to play a small but important part helping a doctor acquaintance of mine in the eradication of Guinea worm. He provided office space, logistical support and large quantities of gauze for water filtration during a lull in the civil war in South Sudan, the last stronghold of the parasite.

Others from Round Table who come to mind include Tony Tilden, one-time banqueting manager to Idi Amin who later set up a company to export Kenyan foodstuffs to the Middle East; Mike Lewis, a dentist who once persuaded me to carry some salvaged gold fillings back to London, making me technically a gold smuggler, and went on to set up a winery and newspaper in northern Canada; and Michael Clifford, whose Craft Industries, producing trinkets and souvenirs for the embryonic tourism industry, bid for and unexpectedly won an order to produce 100,000 identical batiks for Panasonic in Japan.

Erno Parani was large man, a strong and kind gentle giant, originally from Hungary, whom I met after moving on to Skyline. We had won a contract to design and construct the Ghanian stand at the first All-Africa Trade Fair, held in Lagos in 1972, and contracted out the construction to Erno's company. While we were working with Erno, he had occasion to fly to London, travelling with East African Airways. The plane crashed on take-off from Khartoum, where it had made an intermediate stop. Many of the passengers escaped, including Erno, who returned to the aircraft several times to help others. As he finally moved away from the wreck it caught fire and he heard crying. He rushed back into the plane to successfully rescue a child, but suffered terrible burns in doing so. He died in hospital a few days, the last fatality from the crash. It was an extraordinarily act of bravery which deserves to be remembered.

There were of course also the drifters and misfits who wound up in Kenya for one reason or another. Peter Nienstaedt, who had introduced me to Jeff, drifted down from Copenhagen in his red Ford Transit and stayed for a decade or so, at one time unable to leave because, I was told, of unpaid tax bills. He made several attempts to slip away unobtrusively, once in a boat which ran out of fuel on the way to Pemba Island off the coast of Tanzania, once in a light plane which was forced down by mechanical problems. I assume he eventually paid his bills and left legally as he lived in Sussex for many years until his recent death.

Michael Godfrey came to Nairobi to manage a large new hotel, only to have his employment terminated on his first day, apparently because of family politics between the owners. He went on to manage Hunters Lodge on the Mombasa Road, where once a buffalo wandered into his kitchen and did considerable damage, and later Mountain Lodge, on the slopes of Mount Kenya, where my wife Vivienne and I recently spent an enjoyable couple of days.

It was an extraordinarily exciting and stimulating time to be in Kenya among these, and many other, remarkable characters. Between them, these people had a significant influence on how I looked at life, and, I have no doubt, played a part in shaping the person I became.

10. ROUND TABLE

ROUND TABLE IS A YOUNG men's service club, with membership limited to men between the ages of eighteen and forty and an ethos of civic responsibility and fellowship. Each 'Table' was restricted to forty members with not more than two from any single profession. As I write it is almost defunct, but at the time it was thriving, with eighteen Tables in the Association of Round Tables in East Africa, ARTEA, stretching from Mauritius to Uganda and Addis Ababa, with three in Nairobi enjoying friendly rivalry.

While I was working with Jeff our neighbour Ian 'Mitch' Mitchelmore persuaded me to join Nairobi Table Number 1 in 1972. We met twice a month for dinner at the Norfolk Hotel, sometimes adjourning to the Sombrero night club afterwards. Membership was predominantly European and Asian and included some large, boisterous personalities and some serious hardworking professionals; looking back, I remember that the large, boisterous personalities were also serious hardworking professionals, something not always immediately apparent. There were quarterly ARTEA weekend meetings, when the association took over a hotel and fifty or more couples from the region got together to discuss the Association's affairs and to socialize. I attended such quarterly meetings at Kilaguni Lodge in Tsavo, Two Fishes Hotel at Diani Beach, the New Arusha Hotel and the beautiful house of Hatim Karimjee in Tanga; unfortunately I missed those in the Seychelles and Mauritius. They were relaxed weekends, lubricated by alcohol, and new friendships were made with members from across the region.

In addition to our regular dinners we had a number of fundraising events, some regular, some one-offs. We organised charity premieres for several of the James Bond films, a relay pram race from Nairobi to Mombasa, ridiculous games of 'pushball' the object of which was to shove a ball about 6 feet in diameter through the opposing team's goal, and Christmas parties for the Nairobi Barnardo's home. At one of those we re-established contact with William Ireri; when he was about ten he had been moved from the Cheshire Home to Barnado's and we had lost touch for a while - it was a huge delight to suddenly see this slightly crooked face grinning up at me.

I recall playing rugby, a rather more conventional sport than pushball, on the same team as Hamza Kassongo from Dar es Salaam Table. At the time Wales was the top rugby-playing team in the world, and coming off the field I congratulated Hamza, who had played with great flair.

'You must have Welsh blood,' I said.

'No, Scottish actually; my grandparents ate a missionary.'

As well as raising money we donated time. With others I spent a few days helping paint the SOS children's home in Nairobi, and several members regularly spent weekends working at an orphanage and farm in Garissa near the border with Somalia.

The major fundraising effort took place each Christmas and New Year, when the combined Nairobi Tables were donated large chunks of airtime on the local radio and TV. We hosted request programmes, when money was pledged for records played, and televised charity auctions. One year I was one of the

DJs, taking calls and pledges of money, the first time I had been on radio. The event was well established, the demand for music to be played was strong and we were able to ask quite large sums. One young lady couldn't afford the asking price and offered to come in to the studio to pay me in kind, an offer which I politely turned down. When I got home I asked my family what they had thought of my debut. 'Oh,' they said, 'we didn't hear you, we went to the club for a swim.'

In 1975, my last Christmas in Nairobi, this fundraising effort raised £65,000, the equivalent, as I write this in 2022, of more than half a million pounds. These funds paid the entire annual running costs of six mobile units treating trachoma, river blindness. The efforts of a few dozen people giving up their time over Christmas and New Year saved 100,000 people, mainly children, from blindness. It was one of the most worthwhile things – with the best return on effort – with which I have been involved in my entire life, and of course was hugely enjoyable.

Each year we held a large dinner at the New Stanley Hotel, to which we invited the older men of Nairobi Rotary Club. One year, as Speakers' Secretary, I persuaded my friend Dawson Mlamba to be guest speaker. Dawson was Permanent Secretary in the Ministry of Foreign Affairs, Edinburgh-educated, intelligent, excellent company but with a serious alcohol problem. He arrived drunk and proceeded to get thoroughly and, almost literally, legless. When the time came for his talk he was beyond speech.

I hoisted him up, supported him with my arm round his shoulder and delivered my own slightly fanciful twenty-minute talk on Kenyan foreign policy, beginning with 'What Dawson would like to say is …', to an amused but highly sceptical audience. All the while Dawson was smiling benignly, nodding occasionally and frequently threatening to slide under the table.

In one of life's small coincidences which I find so extraordinary, forty-five years later, standing on the tarmac at Lewa Downs air strip north of Mount Kenya, I got talking with the co-pilot of the Cessna Caravan taking us to Samburu. I asked him where he was from.

'My dad's from around here, my mum's from Taita.'

'Forty-five years ago I had a very good friend from Taita, Dawson Mlamba.'

'He was my grandfather!'

In a country of more than 50 million what are the chances, as they say.

Each year, Round Table would man one of the checkpoints for what was then the East African Safari Rally. To my everlasting regret I missed out my first year, having only just joined. That year our checkpoint had been on Marsabit Mountain in the far north. Marsabit, an extinct volcano rising 1,000 metres from the surrounding desert and an oasis of misty rain forest, was home to a magnificent elephant known as Ahmed, with tusks of more than 200 pounds each, long enough for him to rest his huge old head on. Those who manned the checkpoint camped by a lake, and when they got up in the early morning Ahmed was close by, standing in the water. He slowly raised his head and those magnificent tusks came up dripping water in the dawn light, and I wasn't there to see or photograph him.

The next year I did man a checkpoint, just outside the Mara Game Reserve, in which we camped. After three days rallying the cars were very spread out, and we spent the entire day in baking heat, chatting, drinking beer and eating with, just occasionally, the tedium broken when a car roared in and a card was thrust impatiently out of the window for stamping. At that time the rally still had some amateur drivers and I remember a delightful couple, Mr. and Mrs. Shah, who competed regularly. They stopped in a cloud of dust and Mrs. Shah, a mumsy Indian lady in a sari, tumbled out, handbag spilling its contents onto the ground, fumbling, apologetic, shy. We stamped her card and off they roared: I believe they were placed in the top ten that year. They might have appeared amateur but they were superb drivers.

About midnight we closed the checkpoint, all the cars still running having passed, and drove back into the Mara to our camp. There had been heavy rains, the plains were flooded and we met a hippo walking towards us along the road. It was a fairly full moon and I stood my ground, fortified by the bravado of Tusker beer. Fortunately he gave way and wandered off into the surrounding water. I was sharing a tent with a Danish friend, Bent. During the night I had to go out to relieve myself of some of the Tusker beer. I stood outside the tent and peed downwind, staring short-sightedly into the moonlit bush. I imagined I saw a cheetah a few feet away, watching me. As I stumbled back into the tent Bent woke and also went out to pee. The next morning I told him that I had imagined seeing a cheetah: 'Ja, I saw it too,' he said.

When we returned to Nairobi, Bent asked me to drive his big heavy Volvo as he was new to Africa and still nervous on rough roads. The rain had been torrential, and we came to a bridge flooded with about 6 inches of fast-flowing water. Looking back I recognize that my life has been enriched by my sometimes foolhardy optimism. I decided we could get across with my passengers pushing, so I floored the accelerator, soaking those in my wake, and we made it, just. The cars following decided to go back and find a way round the flooded bridge. They arrived back in Nairobi a full two days after we did.

Round Table was hugely supportive if a member had problems. In 1975 Bente suffered an ectopic pregnancy which nearly cost her her life. She lost a great deal of blood and I rushed her, comatose, to Nairobi hospital. They checked her blood group, O positive, told me they had none compatible in their blood bank and suggested I call my friends.

It was midday on a Sunday, and I knew that Round Table friends often congregated at the restaurant at the Golf Range, which belonged to two of them. I called; the waiter who answered knew me (we were also regulars) and I asked him to bring one of my friends to the phone. Michael Clifford came on, I explained the problem and within a couple of hours we had 12 pints of compatible blood donated which, together with a couple of pints of mine, was sufficient to stabilise her. Another table member Norman Guthrie, Big Norm to his many friends, had more serious problems: a major car crash left him almost dead, and over a period of weeks fellow Tablers donated more than 50 pints.

I have many more fond memories of Nairobi Round Table. It gave me a social circle outside my work and was a point of stability while I was on the rollercoaster of my relationship with Jeff. I made friendships which continue to this day, now spanning continents as we all eventually made our separate ways out of East Africa. It is forty-five years since I last saw Clive Miller, who now lives in Adelaide, but we have been in regular communication for that entire time, first by post, latterly by email. Mike Lewis, known affectionately as Louie the Tooth from his profession of dentistry or Don Luigi from his slightly cavalier attitude to the law, now lives in Vancouver; we maintain an active and interesting email correspondence around politics, food and wine and meet occasionally when he visits family here in the UK.

Until he died a few years ago I regularly visited Mike Godfrey in Germany, where he settled with his German wife Ina. He remained a good friend, very supportive of me during difficult periods in my work and personal life, and I last saw him a few years ago for his eightieth birthday, a few months before he died. Michael Clifford returned to the UK a couple of years after us and settled in Winchester, where he bought a shop also serving the tourist market. He became godfather to my youngest daughter, then led a peripatetic life in South Africa and the Far

East before settling in Australia where I visited him in Perth twenty years ago. He is now sadly suffering from dementia; we still correspond but he has reverted to hand-written letters, infrequent and sadly repetitive. When he left the UK I bought his car, a Renault 16. It eventually spontaneously combusted when I re-possessed it from an ex-employee who had refused to hand it back – a long story not relevant to this memoir.

On his return to the UK in 1977 Tony Tilden set up a loose organization of ex-Nairobi Round Table members in the UK, When-we (the conversation at any gathering of old East Africa hands begins, inevitably and predictably, 'When we were in Africa ...'). Meetings were initially at the Penscot Farmhouse, the lovely small Somerset hotel Tony had bought, and ran from Friday evening to Monday morning. The bar was well-stocked with Tusker beer, the company was convivial, the reminiscences continued late into the night and the resulting hangovers were well-earned.

When Tony eventually sold his hotel the tradition continued at other similar country hotels; I no longer attend the annual get-togethers but during the Covid pandemic, which persists as I write, they have been augmented by monthly Zoom meetings, usually with a dozen or so participants. I have joined a few and some enjoyable old memories have been rekindled.

Writing this has led me to muse on friendships and their origins. The British use the word 'friend' very loosely, but in Denmark, where I lived for two years, a definite distinction is made between *ven*, friend, and *bekendt*, acquaintance, and I think the correct use of the two words enhances the value of true friendships. Like most people I have many acquaintances and a few close friends. My friendships fall into three distinct groups: those from my school days; those from East Africa; and those from the period after my first marriage ended. I am bound to the first group by the shared experiences of childhood and little else; to the second by the excitement of our lives as young adults in Africa, memories almost as vivid now as the day they were made; and to the third, most of whom are a generation younger than me, by the common purpose of giving back to life.

On my return to the UK, I transferred my membership to Farnham Round Table which I enjoyed and where I made acquaintances rather than friends: organizing a fireworks display in Farnham Park does not have quite the same bonding effect as dodging hippos in the Mara or dancing on the beach at Diani.

11. THE CLOSING YEARS

NOT LONG AFTER I FIRST arrived in Nairobi while working on the Nairobi Hilton project, I had got to know one of the staff of El Al, a young Danish woman called Louise. She had since married Jim Noon, a pilot in the Flying Doctor service and we would bump into them occasionally at functions organized by the Danish Society. On one such occasion Jim mentioned that he was now employed as company pilot by System Building Services (SBS), a construction company, and that their financial controller was leaving.

My relationship with Jeff was coming to an end and, needing income, I introduced myself. SBS had been set up a few years earlier to build low-cost housing on agricultural estates using a system of lightweight concrete panels cast on site. The innovative system appealed to the frustrated engineer in me, and the three people who had set it up, Patrick Walker, a Nairobi real-estate developed, Stuart Allison, a coffee farmer and Tony Vincent, an accountant – none of them full time with the company, appealed to my inner entrepreneur. They agreed that I would join on a flexible consultancy arrangement, leaving me time to spend on the Holiday Inn development should it unmire itself.

The company used Patrick's office in central Nairobi

for formal meetings, but the main premises were a typical warehouse in the industrial area, with storage for building materials and basic office accommodation. I appropriated an old Peugeot pick-up as my 'company car'. After the high-flying dreams at CDIL it was, I think, a subconscious move to bring myself down to earth, but I enjoyed the unpretentious freedom of driving an anonymous pick-up truck.

SBS had a number of contracts for large-scale housing projects on sugar estates in Kenya, and one in southern Somalia. It was incorporated in the Isle of Man, and operated in Kenya through an established Nakuru-based construction company, Patrickson and Coxon. Shortly after I joined, we bid for and won a World-Bank-funded three million dollar contract to build several hundred houses on an estate at Kilombero in central Tanzania. With the three directors busy on other things, this became my responsibility. It was a relief, and a pleasure, to get stuck into an actual tangible business venture with a realistic chance of success; looking back it was the first time in my life that I had done so.

Under the well-intentioned but misguided presidency of Julius Nyerere the Tanzanian economy was desperate, and day-to-day life in Dar wasn't easy. While we were negotiating to get the contract I had to visit several times, on one occasion taking Bente with me Vehicles were like gold dust, but fortunately my Round Table friend Hamza Kassongo ran the Mercedes dealership and lent me a vehicle he had taken in part-exchange, a Mini Moke, which was a very small open-sided jeep-like vehicle on a Mini chassis.

Another Round Table acquaintance, Andy Chande, was a great Dar-based fixer. We needed all the influence we could get to secure this large contract in a country where we were unknown, so I invited Andy and his wife to join Bente and me for dinner, and arranged to collect them from their house in Oyster Bay. Andy was in his early forties and slightly built. I had not met his wife but as soon as they emerged from the house,

I realised that the Mini Moke, not designed with traditionally built ladies like Jayalaxmi in mind, was not the ideal vehicle. Between us we managed to shoe-horn most of her, clad in an elegant sari, inside, but on the short drive I took particular care on right turns lest her left buttock hit the road. They sensibly took a taxi home.

Forty years later I had coffee with Andy in London; his wife had died and he reminisced about his life. In his very quiet way he had achieved much, in business, philanthropy and as an advisor to the Tanzanian government. He was the first Tanzanian citizen to be given an honorary British knighthood, and when he died a couple of years later most of his very substantial fortune went into his charitable foundation targeting education in East Africa.

Hamza went on to have a successful career in broadcasting and we kept casually in touch. I last saw him a few years ago at a very enjoyable dinner with another Round Table friend, Hatim Karimjee. Hatim, scion of a wealthy family of traders who had settled in what was then the Sultanate of Zanzibar in the middle of the nineteenth century, hosted us at his beautiful house on the beach at Oyster Bay. Hamza had lost none of his exuberance.

SBS as an Isle of Man company it banked in dollars. One of the conditions of the Kilombero contract, which was between World Bank in Washington and SBS in the Isle of Man, was that it would be exempt from any Tanzanian taxes. At that time, under the very extreme socialism imposed by Nyerere, income tax was levied at 100 per cent of any income over £100 per month, with corporate taxes being similarly punitive.

I flew to Dar es Salaam to set up the administration. The first stop was of course the bank; we would be spending a couple of million dollars in Tanzania, much of it in cash for wages and local purchases and we needed a pool of Tanzanian shillings with which to operate. The bank told me that we could not have an account in Tanzania unless the company was registered with the Tanzanian tax authorities; when trying to register I asked whether that meant we would have to pay Tanzanian corporation taxes and was told 'yes, of course'.

So our tax exemption meant we could not register the company. That in turn meant no bank account, so we had to operate entirely in cash, which is why I became a money-launderer. The official rate of exchange at the time was around 7 shillings per dollar, while the black-market rate for cash was more than twice that, so through Patrick Walker's many contacts we were put in touch with an Asian gentleman who owned a sawmill in Tanzania generating significant amounts of cash. We would deposit $50,000 at a time into his account in the Isle of man, and I would call in to his office in Dar es Salaam to collect a large cardboard box stuffed with half-price bank notes. The system operated remarkably smoothly, although there was one nervous moment when my colleague Tony had made the collection for me, driven straight to a hardware store and while shopping inside remembered that he had left his Peugeot 404 pickup unlocked with its windows open and a large and inviting cardboard box sitting on the front seat. He rushed outside and fortunately it was still there.

Over the course of the contract, we made more profit from our currency dealing than we did from the construction: I would argue, perhaps without too much conviction, that we had no choice. Regardless, we left behind several hundred decent small houses, of a standard not usually enjoyed by agricultural workers in East Africa.

We recruited six British expats, most of them old Africa hands, to supervise the building works beginning with the construction of six small bungalows for themselves, which would eventually house the management of the sugar plantation. They in turn recruited some 400 labourers from the local population and work got underway. I got to know Kilombero well: for the remainder of my time in East Africa I visited the site at least once a week.

The company had two planes. The first was an ageing

Cessna 182, an airborne *matatu* the door of which would, on occasion, open unexpectedly at 10,000 feet. It was alarming but not dangerous, as we were strapped in and the slipstream would slam it shut again. The second was a rather newer Cessna 210, single-engined with a retractable undercarriage and considerably faster, which we used for longer flights. I would call Jim Noon the evening before and we would meet at Wilson Airport just after dawn. He would do the take-off, then get out his book and hand control over to me, with the simple instruction to leave Kilimanjaro to the right.

I would give control back to Jim when Kilimanjaro, soaring thousands of feet higher than our maximum altitude, was safely behind us and the Indian Ocean in sight. Our approach to Dar es Salaam airport was over the sea, sparkling in the early morning sunlight, its surface dotted with traditional dug-out fishing canoes each with its single off-white lateen sail, their outriggers lifted out of the water by the force of our backdraft. After landing, an insignificant speck of a plane on the runway built for large jets, we taxied to the terminal where we cleared customs.

We would usually spend a few hours in Dar es Salaam, either with the World-Bank appointed Dutch consultant engineer responsible for monitoring our progress and certifying our applications for payment, or with our local agent Cesare, a building contractor Tanzanian born but of Italian origin, whose office we used. Cesare helped to us source materials and looked after the substantial amounts of cash which we used for purchases and took to the site for wages in the small portable safe fitted in the plane.

Our route on to Kilombero took us over the wonderful Selous Game Reserve, the largest yet one of the least-known of all the many game reserves in Africa. Being far away from any regular flight paths Jim would take us down to about two hundred feet and I would watch, entranced, as the herds of giraffe and antelope scattered below us. Jim had learned his bush pilot skills with the flying doctor service, when at times he would be called upon to land on a dirt road or a beach or a dry riverbed, so the short dirt strip at Kilombero was easy for him. Landing only needed a heavy foot on the brakes, but take-off was made more challenging by the row of gum trees at the upwind end. It was full throttle, no flaps and, just when it seemed inevitable that we would pile into the trees, flaps down and the little plane would hop up over them and head back north-east to Dar es Salaam; disconcerting the first couple of times but I got used to it.

As there were at the time shortages of many foodstuffs in Tanzania, we would bring down in the safe goodies unavailable in Dar as a low-level bribe for the consultant engineer – bacon, butter and the Marmite to which he appeared addicted. The safe was then refilled with cash for the site wages. Flying in a small plane over the plains of Africa with the heat of the sun bouncing back from the hard-baked earth can be bumpy and after one such flight when we unpacked the cash we found that a jar of Marmite left in the safe had smashed. Wages that week were paid in Marmite-soaked bank notes.

There was another food incident that had a more lasting effect. At the request of Cesare I had brought with me a pack of butter, of which Dar had an ongoing shortage. He collected me from the airport and, on the way to his office, I put the butter in the glove compartment. He forgot about it, the tropical sun did its thing and for the rest of its life his vehicle reeked of rancid butter.

Later on, as we got organised, the site manager would drive the three-hundred-mile round trip to Dar to collect the wages. One week there was a hitch in the money-laundering arrangements and no cash was available, so four hundred angry workers rioted. The six expat staff fled to Dar in their Range Rovers and called me in Nairobi to get the problem sorted.

Jim and I flew straight to the site and were met by four hundred very angry men led by the foreman Odinga was a long-time employee whom I knew, English speaking and a trouble-making rogue, but we had always got on. We parlayed for about an hour, in the open under a hot sun, gradually defusing the situation until I judged it time to suggest a return to work, which I did, tactlessly, by saying 'Okay, let's not stand around talking like a lot of old women, and get back to work.'

Odinga smiled at me then turned to the others and said in Swahili: 'The bwana is calling you all old women.' Uproar, four hundred men stoop down to pick up stones.

It was one of those 'Oh, shit' moments. I did some fast talking and eventually, after another hour or so, calm was restored, Jim and I flew back to Nairobi and the management returned from Dar.

With the panels of lightweight concrete used to construct the houses at Kilombero being cast on site, the supply of cement was always a problem. All of Tanzania relied on a single cement factory in Dar es Salaam, where lorries would queue for several days to get their allocation, and we needed a total of a thousand tons. We also had tight time constraints with heavy penalties for late delivery, so an alternative source was essential. Fortunately there was a cement factory in neighbouring Zambia with some available; our site was close to the TanZam Railway which had recently opened and linked land-locked Zambia with the port at Dar es Salaam, so delivery from Lusaka seemed logistically straightforward.

We ordered our thousand tonnes for immediate delivery, but after a month nothing had arrived. Jim and I flew south-west following the railway line and eventually found the train, abandoned in a siding towards the Zambian border. A few phone calls and we finally got our precious cement. Operating in Africa was always interesting.

The railway was a prestige project, one of the early examples of Chinese investment into black Africa. In addition to freight there was one passenger train a day in each direction. It was single track with a few passing points, but when it reached

Dar es Salaam it divided into half a dozen separate tracks just so the impressive new terminus could have multiple and unnecessary platforms. The spending of aid money is not always as well targeted as it should be.

For the occasions when we had to stay over in Dar, we had rented a small villa in Oyster Bay just north of town, where we also kept a car. Looking back, I loved the easy access we had to things, cars, houses, aeroplanes; but the privileged life enjoyed by almost all white expatriates has had long-lasting effects on post-colonial society. During the colonial era it was unusual for the routine work of the civil service to be entrusted to indigenous people, and the often quite pedestrian administrators required to do it could only be tempted to exchange their familiar surroundings in Europe for a new life in the far-flung colonies by the offer of a very comfortable lifestyle. When independence came the indigenous people who replaced them understandably expected the same, putting a totally unnecessary burden on the economy and creating needless divisions in society.

SBS also negotiated a contract to build similar low-cost houses on the outskirts of Lagos and again it fell to me to sort out the administrative and financial arrangements. Work at Kilombero was almost complete and a couple of the expat staff transferred to Lagos, renting a comfortable villa in which I stayed on my only visit.

It was a wild time in Nigeria: the city was awash with money from the fairly newly discovered oil in the Niger Delta, construction was booming and building materials, particularly cement, were in short supply. It was a time when scores of ships were anchored offshore, waiting their turn to enter the crowded port and discharge. Corruption was of course rife, but if we hadn't gone along with it our houses would not have been built. In their own peculiarly Nigerian way, there was a strange code of honour among the corrupt officials. A ship loaded with cement arrived for us and anchored offshore. Our site manager Tony visited the harbour master and was told that it would cost

$20,000 to get the ship unloaded; Tony returned with twenty $1,000 notes and to ensure 'good faith' the harbour master cut them in half and returned half to Tony, who gave them back a couple of days later after our badly needed cement had been delivered.

When I arrived for my short visit I was given a handful of grubby Naira notes and told by the bookkeeper, who technically reported to me, that I didn't need to account for them. As an ex-auditor I really didn't approve, but as a pragmatist I decided to go along with the system. There was little to spend the money on apart from the odd beer at a bar in the evening, and my assistant in Nairobi was sufficiently astute to make sure no-one over-exploited the system.

In the evenings we would sometimes have a drink at a nearby bar, one which tried to set itself apart from the others and tempt in the higher-spending expatriates by maintaining a better dress code. In the widely spoken local pidgin the khaki shorts worn by most European expatriates were 'knicker'; this bar had prominent notices stating 'Saturday night No Knickers'.

A huge programme of road building was underway to cope with the ever-growing traffic, and driving was chaos. The airport was less than 10 miles from the city centre and while the journey could be completed in an hour or so, it could just as often take six hours. Prudent visitors booked on a morning flight would get to the airport the night before. For an evening flight you allocated the entire day for the taxi ride.

My best memories from that trip are, surprisingly, culinary. Tony had engaged a cook/house boy from Benin and, as I had found in Madagascar, the French had left their colonies with significantly better culinary traditions than the British. Each morning the grilled tomatoes accompanying our breakfast were dressed with the finest sliver of onion, a small detail but typical of the care he took in preparing our meals. It was in a bar in Lagos that I first tasted satay, unknown in Kenya and rare at the time in the UK, but ubiquitous as a snack in the bars of Lagos.

Eventually the work at Kilombero was completed and my role reverted to that of financial controller on the three or four other contracts SBS had in progress. I had hugely enjoyed running a major project with the very visible end product of a small housing estate, and dealing with the significant challenges its construction had thrown up, all of which we had overcome. Returning to regular office work had little appeal, and I knew that my time in Africa was coming to an end. I was ready for another challenge.

12. MOVING ON

AFTER NEARLY NINE YEARS IN Kenya I realised that the great satisfaction I had found in my work was likely to diminish, and Bente was becoming increasingly restless, finding involvements with various charities no longer sufficiently challenging. She worked briefly with Rita Larsen, who had the Kenya agency for Carmen hair curlers, but decided that commercial life was not for her. Bente had left school in Denmark at the age of sixteen, never encouraged by her traditionally minded parents to do anything other than routine clerical work, and while in Kenya had used the leisure time available to expatriate wives to study for an A Level in Sociology, which she passed comfortably. From then on she decided her future would be back in the UK, where there were many more opportunities to develop her new-found interests.

I have lived and worked as an expatriate in Denmark, East Africa, the Arabian Gulf and the Caribbean and always found the work both challenging and stimulating. The wives of expatriates (and in those days it was almost always the husband whose career-choices took a couple abroad) have a different experience, often not finding the same fulfilment. Towards the end of our time in Kenya Bente was interviewed on that subject by a journalist from a major UK women's magazine. In the interview she described Nairobi as a 'fools' paradise'; seen from outside I can understand that is how it would have appeared, but having lived and enjoyed that life for nine years I knew it to be an over-simplification. Yes, I and almost all those I knew, had been living a wonderfully cushioned existence, but we had also worked hard and in most cases given back significantly to the community. Post-independence Kenya was thriving and one of the reasons was the hard work and creativeness of the various expatriate communities.

Regardless, I accepted that the time had come to move back to the UK. Marina was ten, Margaret nearly eight, and while there were excellent primary schools in Nairobi we thought that a secondary school in the UK would better equip them for life in Europe. Also, much as I loved my life in Africa, career-wise it was time to move on.

I negotiated a six-month contract to represent SBS in the UK, based in the Caversham offices of Associated Portland Cement, the suppliers of the Cheecolite used to make our light-weight concrete panels, after which I intended to set up a professional accountancy practice, and Bente went back to the UK to buy a house and find a suitable school for our daughters, settling on the small town of Farnham in south west Surrey. She came back for a few weeks to say her final goodbyes before heading off to set up our new home, leaving Marina and Margaret with me – they were due to join her a couple of weeks later.

I negotiated a six-month contract to represent SBS in the UK, based in the Caversham offices of Associated Portland Cement, the suppliers of the Cheecolite used to make our light-weight concrete panels, after which I intended to set up a professional accountancy practice.

My last visit to Kilombero was my last long drive in East Africa. With my two daughters and our house girl Mary I drove one of the company's Peugeot 504s down to Mombasa then south across the border to the lovely little coastal town of Tanga for one of the quarterly weekend meetings of Round Table. With a number of others we stayed in the palatial house of Hatim Karimjee, where he lived before moving to Dar es Salaam. I found out that he was a fellow old Harrovian and, whereas I had been threatened with expulsion, he actually had been expelled, although he claimed not to remember the reason.

We spent a long relaxing weekend, fishing and enjoying good company before driving the six hours south to Dar es Salaam, where we stayed in the Oyster Bay villa. From there it was another twelve hours to Kilombero with an overnight stay at a small riverside lodge. Jim had flown down the previous evening, and he brought Mary and my daughters back to Nairobi, Mary's first flight in a small plane.

I wandered round the little modern village which had been created from virgin bush, tarmac roads with 700 neat one- and two-room units, each with basic kitchen and bathroom, a huge improvement on traditional agricultural housing. I had a few beers with the half dozen expatriates I had come to know well, a couple of whom would later work for me in Portugal, and left at dawn the next day.

The drive to Arusha skirted the Selous game reserve before heading north-west past Moshi, with Kilimanjaro and Mt. Meru looming large on my right. I stayed at the New Safari Hotel, slightly more run-down than it had been on my first visit years before. The final leg back to Nairobi was a nostalgic retracing of my first African road trip; there was a little more traffic and fewer wild animals to be seen, but the road was unchanged, still mostly rough and unmade with some interesting dongas to be navigated. I stopped for a beer at Namanga River Lodge, sat in the shade of the lovely old acacia trees and thought back on nine wonderful years.

A couple of days later I put Marina and Margaret on a plane back to England. As I watched them follow the hostess confidently through the check in, not bothering to look back, hand in hand and each with her own little suitcase, I thought back to our arrival almost exactly nine years earlier. I knew that Africa had given them a good start to life, and it was their time too to move on.

Our house in Peponi Road had been bought in my name with CDIL's money. I reckonedthe company owed me at least its modest value for the enormous time and effort I had put in over several years, so I tried to sell it. Jeff got an injunction to stop me. I was seriously concerned that he would also try to prevent me leaving the country, so I flew to Dar es Salaam, and from there direct to London.

I would love to have left with a little more fanfare, to have had a joyful end to what had been, by and large, a hugely enjoyable period of my life, but sometimes you have to take what life does to you. I knew I would be back but was ready to leave, already making plans for what I would do next. Furtively, by the back door of Dar, I slipped away.

I returned to Kenya on SBS business a few months later and met Jeff at the Muthaiga Club. He was by then drinking very heavily and we had a brief conversation. His last words to me were 'I hope our paths never cross again.' They never did.

A couple of years later, Gulzaar phoned to tell me that Jeff had died of a heart attack. I wept, long and hard. He was a huge personality, a man of enormous energy and potential, a man with, quite literally, fatal flaws, including what I think was an inbuilt self-destruct mechanism, the product of his damaging childhood. We had been the closest of friends and then I became his greatest enemy, but in those years I had loved him.

Some years afterwards I was driving through the desert in Eastern Saudi Arabia in the late afternoon, when the sand dunes are at their sinuous best, and I felt his presence beside me, his arm comfortable around my shoulders. Although I no longer believe in an afterlife in which individuals exist, I knew that he had forgiven me for whatever I had done, or perhaps forgiven himself for what he had done, and that he was, posthumously, once again my friend.

13. AN AFRICAN FAMILY

WHEN NJOROGE INTRODUCED HIMSELF TO us as our 'shamba boy' on the day we arrived in our first Nairobi home, he proudly showed me an employment book going back to 1935. That was when he had started working for Philip Johnson, the Gill and Johnson partner who had built the flats. Njoroge was a wrinkled old Kikuyu, lacking many of his teeth, and during the twenty-five years we knew him he never seemed to change or age.

Within a matter of days, Njoroge's daughter Jane Njeri, 'Jeannie', was also installed as our house girl. There were six flats in our small block and the servants' quarters comprised three small double rooms. Here, sixteen-year-old Jeannie was required to share a room with a man. We thought this unacceptable, so she moved in with us, living in our small spare room. There were still some old-school white Kenyans who, behind our backs, expressed surprise at this. One remark relayed back to us was 'I've heard that miners in Zambia sometimes have servants living in their house.' White Kenyans, many of whom were from upper-middle-class British backgrounds and came to Kenya to farm, considered themselves superior to white Zambians, who arrived as working miners. Much more insidious pressure was exerted by the other servants, and eventually it was Jeannie herself who said she would prefer to live in the servants' quarters, sharing with a man called Paul.

A couple of days before our second Christmas in Nairobi, after I had left for work, Jeannie came into our bedroom and, to my wife's great surprise, sat down heavily on the edge of the bed complaining of very severe stomach pains. My wife drove her straight to hospital where, a few hours later, she gave birth to a little boy who, unsurprisingly, bore a very strong resemblance to Paul. The birth was very premature and sadly, or perhaps fortunately, the baby only survived a few days. We had remarked that Jeannie had been putting on weight but attributed it to her very healthy appetite. From then on we insisted that she live in the flat with us.

During the four years she worked for us Jeannie was part house-girl and part *ayah* – nanny – to our daughters. She came with us on some of our days out, and a couple of times we took her down to the coast. I recall the first time she saw the sea: standing at the top of the beach she gazed in wonder out over the Indian Ocean, unmoving for many minutes, lost in its immensity. The first time I suggested she try one of the lobsters we would buy from the fishermen on the beach she responded, 'I'm not going to eat that *dudu*', *dudu* being the Swahili catch-all word for insects and creepie-crawlies.

Jeannie was an intelligent young woman, but having had only a rudimentary education there were few opportunities open to her. It was a source of great satisfaction that we were able to support her into evening classes and a job at Skyline, and it was there that she met and fell in love with one of our drivers, Samuel. In 1972 they married; Marina and Margaret, then aged six and three, were bridesmaids at their wedding.

Njoroge lived, together with most of his family, on a one-acre plot at Banana Hill, 10 miles outside Nairobi, and when we had visitors from Europe I would take them out to meet him so they could see a typical African home. On the small plot there were several corrugated iron dwellings surrounded by well-kept vegetable patches which, with the few chickens and goats wandering around, provided most of the food for the family. Whenever we visited he would not allow us to leave empty-handed, giving us some eggs, corn cobs or papaya and, on one occasion, just as we were about to drive off thrusting a live chicken in through the car window. My young daughters immediately gave it a name, from memory I think it was Horatio, and of course once you have named an animal it is impossible to eat it. Having no facilities in our flat to keep a chicken we donated it to the house boys.

Njoroge was uneducated but wise, and he and I would have long discussions on local politics. On one occasion when I visited him, a couple of years after we had moved back to the UK, he was complaining about the corruption of local politicians and civil servants. He asked me whether I thought it was possible that the British administration could return as, in his view, back in the colonial days governance had been better. I last saw him in 1987 when I was on holiday with my family, the last Kenya holiday I was to have with my father-in-law Boddy. Njoroge died in 1992, probably some seventy-five years old. Now, more than fifty years after I first met him I have very similar conversations with his son-in-law Samuel – the main topic remains the corruption of local politicians.

For years after leaving Africa I kept in touch with Njoroge's family, sending Christmas cards and the occasional letter, and writing to Jeannie care of the school in the village to which she and Samuel had moved as she did not have her own post office box, but eventually, getting no replies, I stopped. Then, in 2010, a dozen years after our last contact, I visited Nairobi on an assignment for a small charity, Africa First, and asked them if they could trace her through the village school.

They eventually managed to do so, and passed on her phone number after I got back to the UK. To her surprise and delight, I called her. We corresponded for a couple of years and caught up with what her family had become. She and Samuel had had five children, three boys and two girls. Tragically one of their sons, Peter, had been killed in a car accident a year or so earlier. Peter's wife Faith was unable to look after their two children and Jeannie's younger daughter, also called Faith, a delightful and resourceful woman who makes a fairly precarious living selling jewellery to tourists on the streets of Nairobi, took over responsibility for them.

The following year I decided to visit them and combine it with a holiday in Tanzania with Vivienne. I went out to Nairobi a few days before Vivienne, and when I landed early in the morning Jeannie was at the airport to meet me, a short and stout fifty-five-year-old grandmother. With her were her daughter Faith and four of her grandchildren, Esther, Jane Njeri, Samuel and Simon. They were shy at first – I was probably the first European they have ever interacted with – and greeted me with handshakes; from Jeannie I got a long and warm hug. I have no words for what this meant to me, or to them. Jeannie had looked after my two older children when they were new-formed and vulnerable, and she was a quiet but important part of our lives in Kenya. She had matured into a thoughtful, intelligent and dignified peasant farmer. I had never expected to see her again and as I say, I have no words – it was one of life's very special moments.

I picked up my hire car, a small, solid 4x4, and we drove to the hotel they had chosen for me, the Blue Springs on the Thika Road. As they say, you get what you pay for, and the room rate was £10.50 per night (paid in cash, daily, in advance). To describe it as adequate is possibly an exaggeration, but it would have been churlish to have moved out straight away.

We lazed around drinking tea and were joined by Jeannie's oldest daughter Alice (mother of Esther and Simon), her husband, who had a good job in the police, and Faith, the widow of Peter and mother of Jane and Samuel. After lunch I drove Jeannie, both Faiths, Esther, Jane and Samuel (in my four-seater car, seat belts being something of a formality in Kenya) to Faith's flat where I read a little to the children and looked at their school work. There is something very special about reading to young children and by then their shyness was evaporating. I got such pleasure from small brown hands insinuating themselves into mine and little children snuggling up as I read in a language that the smallest didn't understand.

We then drove out to Jeannie and Samuel's smallholding in the village of Gacharage, a dozen bumpy miles past Thika. The roads were the worst I had ever driven on and the driving style took a bit of getting used to. My only major mistake, and almost my last, was, in following Faith's directions, to drive the wrong way up a one-way road and meet a phalanx of very large lorries coming the other way, unwilling (and possibly unable) to stop. I made the instant decision to test the off-road capabilities of my little car – luckily they were okay. At the time Faith did not drive and I rapidly learnt to take her directions with a degree of caution.

The smallholding is in an idyllic setting, four acres on a hillside in fertile, rolling country, lush green interlaced with a network of red murram roads. At the top sits a ramshackle corrugated iron dwelling of four rooms with separate huts for cooking and toilet, a few hutches for rabbits, and a small makeshift shelter for the cow. The main room has well-worn sofas around three walls, a fireplace at the end and a large low table in the middle with just enough room for circulation. Prominent on one wall is a faded old colour photo of my two oldest daughters as bridesmaids at Jeannie and Samuel's wedding forty years ago.

On this plot Jeannie and Samuel grow coffee, macadamia nuts, bananas and avocados, which they sell, and the usual staples, maize, yams, beans and greens, to feed themselves; scrawny chickens peck around in the dust and the cow's milk is collected each morning by a local dairy, providing much of their cash income.

I said hello to Samuel, who I hadn't seen for thirty-five years and who had matured into a quiet, wise and dignified man, and to their youngest son Martin, slow-witted, with no doubt a diagnosable syndrome but why bother diagnosing it as nothing could be done? Martin potters inoffensively round the shamba and, as is the way in Africa, is completely accepted and cared for by the village community.

That evening, Faith and I drove back to the hotel, from where she took a Matatu back to her flat. I had dinner – a chicken curry, the chicken involved having led a very long and, one hopes, happy life, washed down with a couple of welcome cold Tusker beers – to the repetitive, insistent and hypnotic beat of the African band in the bar next door. Before going up to my room I checked out the 200 or so people (it was a Saturday night) in the restaurant and bar and, as I suspected, I was the only non-African in the place. In spite of the idiosyncrasies of the hotel I slept like a baby: it had been a long, exhausting and emotional twenty-four hours.

The following day Faith met me at the hotel and we again drove out to Gacharage. While the women prepared lunch, Samuel and I went for a walk to the local coffee factory about half a mile away, stopping to chat to friends and neighbours along the way. Forty years rolled away and I was drinking tea with his father-in-law Njoroge, discussing politics and farming and generally putting the world to rights. A couple of chickens were despatched to make the lunch, cooked on two charcoal braziers, and everything we ate, apart from the rice, had been grown within 100 yards of where we sat. Most of the family were there, some neighbours dropped in to say hello and we had a relaxed day.

For the first leg of the journey back to the hotel there were ten in the car, including two behind the back seat. The only major driving error was going the wrong way round a roundabout, again directed by Faith, who had the careless acceptance of non-drivers that everything was going to be fine. I was less worried when I realised that half a dozen other cars had followed us. I dropped everyone at their various flats in the suburbs of Nairobi, found my way back to the hotel and had a relaxing evening, musing on the day, which had reminded me why I think that rural Kenyans living in the rich and fertile parts of the country are among the most contented people I have met.

Day three was lovely, lovely but long. Faith came to the hotel at 7.30 and we drove up to Gacharage to collect Jeannie, Samuel and Martin. From there we drove to the land near Nanyuki where Samuel's mother lives and farms, with the help of their older son Anthony. Samuel said the drive would take an hour but this proved a serious underestimate. Two and a half hours later we arrived. A long but easy drive to a beautiful place, 100 acres bordering the forests of Mount Kenya, quite remote and peaceful. It is arid country, but there is a small dam which never dries, its water piped from the Aberdare mountains to the west.

All the others had driven there separately, and it was the first gathering of the whole family for years. A young goat was slaughtered for the occasion, and it amused me that although Kikuyu men are quite uninvolved in cooking and domestic matters, when it comes to barbecues they take over, just like their counterparts in the UK. The results however were excellent; I was given a rack of ribs and a sharp knife and while most of the family ate outside in the sunshine I ate, formally but companionably, in the living room with Samuel's mother Peninah, eightyish and still going strong, an old freedom fighter who had been imprisoned with Jomo Kenyatta. Communication was limited to smiles, nods and the occasional grunt of satisfaction with the food.

I had become '*Guka*' (Kikuyu for 'Grandad') to the children, and spent much of the time playing with them. They took me the few hundred yards to Anthony's house, a glorious walk through open countryside, a few scrawny cattle grazing, gazelles sheltering under the occasional acacia thorns, the towering peaks of Mount Kenya rising up on one side and the Aberdares hazy in the distance on the other. The temperature was a pleasant 25 degrees and I was reminded yet again of why I love East Africa.

I had planned to leave at 3.00 but everyone was having such a great time I couldn't hurry them, so we left at 5.30. This meant a very stressful journey back: driving after dark in Kenya you take your life in your hands. I finally made it to the hotel at 9.45, and slept the sleep of happy exhaustion.

The following day I moved in to central Nairobi, staying at the Hilton Hotel, a considerable improvement on the Blue Springs on the Thika Road. Jeannie and Faith joined me for lunch, and I spent a relaxed afternoon re-acquainting myself with the city. Early the next morning I drove to the airport and delivered back the by now very dusty hire car. I met Vivienne off her flight from London and we flew to Dar es Salaam for the first of many holidays we have enjoyed together in East Africa. It had been a wonderful few days, and I resolved to keep in touch and to help this lovely and hospitable family in any way I could.

Ever since that visit Jeannie has phoned me regularly, probably half a dozen times a year. International calls on the Kenyan mobile networks are extraordinarily cheap, about two pence per minute, a tiny fraction of what we, the exploited consumers of Western Europe, have to pay. Given that the cost of the infrastructure cannot be significantly different. the UK regulators allow mobile phone service providers to make obscenely large profits. Vodafone, one of the first, went from a standing start to become one of the most profitable companies in the country in a very short period of time, early investors doing extremely well. In contrast, one of the early African telecoms entrepreneurs, Mo Ibrahim, philanthropic by nature, kept charges low and affordable by ordinary Africans. He introduced a staff share-ownership scheme and when he sold his company for more than $3 billion, used much of the proceeds to set up a charitable foundation.

On one of her calls Jeannie told me that their cow had died, a significant loss to their cash income. I bought them another, which shortly after produced a calf, eventually not only doubling their milk production but producing gas for cooking using a simple cow-dung-fed methane digester. We have much to learn from the low-tech ingenuity of developing nations.

Since then I have been back many times. A year or so after that first visit I undertook to pay for the education of the grandchildren, for whom Faith identified a good small private primary school in the town of Mwea, about 50 miles from Gacharage. Initially the four children of school age, two girls both called Jane Njeri and two boys, Simon and Samuel, went; they have been joined in later years by three younger ones. On Vivienne's first visit to Kenya in 2012 she and I spent a day at the school. We were the first Europeans to visit, the rice-growing area round Mwea being far from any tourism activity, and were warmly greeted by the headmistress, accompanied by 'our' four children. She had arranged for us to spend twenty minutes with each class, talking to them about the importance of schooling and indeed anything else which came to mind.

It was a day of delights: the children were bright, self-assured and inquisitive, asking intelligent questions and obviously enjoying their schooling. For most of them we were the first Europeans they had met; some were of course shy but for the majority the excitement of having foreigners come to the school overcame that. One little boy insisted on rubbing Vivienne's skin to see if the colour would come off, and several wanted to run their fingers through my soft white hair.

We had lunch with the headmistress and some of the staff, after which all the children were gathered together in the large and dusty school yard where they sang and performed a short play for us. At the end we were presented with a 10 kilo bag of local rice which, given the weight restrictions on our flight home we gave to Jeannie. A lovely day which gave me hope for the future of the country: African children are, of course, as intelligent and ambitious as any, and Kenya is developing a growing educated middle class which hopefully will eventually put restraints on its corrupt politicians.

From Mwea we went on to Mutira, the secondary school where the older Jane Njeri had been for a year or so. it was very different to the cheerful atmosphere of the Mwea Brethren school, with strict security which, I suppose, is necessary in an institution housing several hundred teenage girls. Although expected we were kept waiting for twenty minutes before we met the headmistress, who made it plain that there was no way we could see the accommodation or classrooms. We said a brief hello to Jane, by then fifteen and obviously enjoying her studies, and left, impressed by the school's record, with 75 per cent of the girls going on to university but feeling rather like parents whose visit was tolerated but not particularly welcome.

Fortunately the school has lived up to its academic reputation. Jane was consistently at or near to the top of her class. In her last year she was chosen, as one of the dozen most gifted students in the whole country, to spend a week at State House in Nairobi being taken to see the legislature, law courts and other government departments for an overview of the machinery of government. As I write this, she is just completing her first semester at Jomo Kenyatta University, where she is studying for a degree in mechanical engineering.

A few years after I re-established contact with Jeannie, I invited her to visit us in the UK. Easier said than done! In order to visit she needed a tourist visa, the issue of which is absolutely routine for the huge majority of the many millions of tourists visiting the UK each year, but for a grandmother from rural Africa the process took a year. It included a couple of humiliating interviews which Jeannie had to attend in Nairobi, interviews at which she was told that she really couldn't expect to be issued with a visa as there was no guarantee that she would return to Kenya!

The letter of refusal from the Entry Clearance Officer (ECO) stated 'Whilst I accept that your sponsor intends to fund your visit, it is your intentions and circumstances I must consider...I am not satisfied that you are residing in settled economic circumstances that represent a reason to leave the UK'.

Imagine, please, this simple elderly African peasant, who has been offered an unimaginable treat by a friend of more than forty years standing who is in the fortunate position of being able to do such things, being told by a jealous white lady at the British High Commission that it is out of the question because there is no guarantee that she would want to return to her loving family and comfortable rural life, and tell me that there isn't institutionalised racism in the British Home and Foreign Offices!

After the first refusal I wrote:

'You state that our right of appeal is limited to section 84(1)(c), which refers only to the Human Rights Act. However the act gives various other grounds for appeal and we are appealing under sub paragraph (f), that the person taking the decision should have exercised differently a discretion conferred by immigration rules.

'The second paragraph of The Decision queries my friend's status as a farmer, partly on the grounds that there are few transactions showing on her bank statement and partly on the (mistaken) assumption that she holds no land or property. My friend, in her own words, is a peasant farmer: as such she operates in an almost exclusively cash economy. This should not mean that she doesn't have the same rights to travel enjoyed by those in other occupations. She and her husband, who incidentally I introduced to each other nearly 40 years ago, have owned a small coffee farm at Gacharage since at least the mid '70s when I first visited it. I was last there in July this year and can assure you it is still in their ownership and is actively farmed. In addition they own some 42 hectares near Nanyuki which is tended by Mrs Gathirwa's mother-in-law.

'That paragraph concludes "I am not satisfied that you

are residing in settled economic circumstances that represent a reason to leave the UK". I cannot of course guess why the examiner should make such assumptions but ask you to question why a grandmother in her 60s who has been married for nearly 40 years, lived in the same house for most of that time, has children, grandchildren, two plots of land and livestock, should not be considered 'settled'.

'As I said in my letter of invitation, I will be responsible for all her expenses while she is in the UK. You can easily check my credentials: I am on the Councils of the United Kingdom Overseas Territories Conservation Forum and Minority Rights Group International, both of which are well known to the FCO, and I was until a few years ago the UK representative of the Government of the Turks and Caicos Islands, in which capacity I met regularly with officials of the FCO. I confirm that I will be responsible for all Mrs. Gathirwa's expenses in the UK and will of course ensure that she returns to Kenya.'

The visa was once more refused on the grounds that I was not a family member. I replied as follows:

'I note that apparently if I were a family member I would have Full Right of Appeal. That is nowhere explained in the regulations, which simply refer to Grounds of Appeal. As her host, inviter and guarantor it seems logical that I should be able to petition on her behalf.

'You say that the application from Mrs Gathirwa contained very little information regarding her claimed circumstances here in Kenya. As I understand it she was not asked if she could substantiate what to her is beyond question: the ECO may not have been satisfied on the evidence presented that Mrs Gathirwa owned property and had any monthly income to live off here in Kenya, but did not ask for additional evidence before deciding to refuse the application.

'I also find it a little surprising that her financial circumstances in Kenya should cause the ECO to assume that, as a settled grandmother who has never left Kenya and has got by quite well for 61 years, she should have any intention of not returning. I'm sorry to labour this point but if you yourself had met Mrs. Gathirwa you would understand how completely absurd that idea is.

'Reading between the lines I suspect that you would agree with me that an error of judgment may have been made and the only barrier to the issue of the visa is bureaucracy. If this is so, there must be room for a review of the decision. If you yourself do not have the authority to do this I would be very grateful if you could pass the papers to someone who has.'

Jeannie's visa was finally issued.

I was at Heathrow to meet her early in the morning of 2 August 2012, having armed her with a letter for the immigration officers with my mobile number should she have difficulty, but after a long wait she emerged through the swing doors, the last passenger through, in her Sunday best dress shimmering with red and gold, looking tired but happy. One of the many things I admire about Jeannie is her equanimity, her ability to take things in her stride. However she did show occasional surprise, the first being when we drove along the M3 on our way to Farnham where I was to leave her for a couple of days with Bente. I noticed she was looking increasingly puzzled and finally she asked, looking at the motorway verges, 'Where are all the people?'

She spent a couple of days with Bente, enjoying joyous, and tearful, reunions with Marina and Maggie, who she last saw as ten- and eight-year-old schoolgirls and who are now women in their mid-forties, then a few days with me in Hampshire where I lived at the time. She is a committed Christian and was overawed by Winchester Cathedral, which I confess also overawes me, an atheist. As an aside, being an atheist does not mean I lack a sense of spirituality. While I do not believe in the existence of a god I recognise that religious practices performed over many centuries leave their imprint on the stones which impassively observe them; it takes a very committed cynic to stand in the Temple of Karnak in Egypt, Shankh monastery in Mongolia or indeed Winchester Cathedral in the UK, and not feel awed.

I drove Jeannie down to Clinnicks, our house in Cornwall, where we were joined by Maggie and her family, and where we watched some of the Olympic games taking place in London that year, cheering on the Kenyan athletes. Jeannie and I went to a church service in the fifteenth-century St Petroc's church in nearby Bodmin, where the appearance of an elderly African lady in a flamboyant red and gold dress was met by barely concealed incredulity. After the service we were shown a rather excessive compensatory welcome and offered refreshments, but we made our excuses and left. Cornwall is not especially racist but visits by African tourists are few and unexpected.

We finished Jeannie's visit with a couple of days in London, seeing most of the favourite tourist places from the top of an open bus. She took it all with her usual calm until we rode the London Eye when I noticed she seemed to become agitated, almost unhappy. I asked what the matter was, and with a slight tone of bitterness she said, 'Why can your people build all this, and we cannot?'

I pointed out that 'my people' had had the huge advantage of hundreds of years of education whereas Kenya had not, and also that our harsher climate had necessitated development of buildings and technology to cope: when Africa has had a few more generations of education she too will create wonders.

Eventually I took Jeannie back to Heathrow. She had enjoyed her visit, and learned much from it, and was of course greatly looking forward to returning to the familiarity of her life in Kenya. Unlike the ladies at the High Commission in Nairobi, she is wise enough to know that affluence and technology are of far less importance than a contented and self-sufficient family life.

Faith continues to be a wonderful auntie to her many nieces and nephews, and we communicate regularly regarding their education. She now has a small shop in central Nairobi which she hopes, when tourism recovers from the Covid pandemic, will provide sufficient income that she can begin to contribute to the school fees.

We plan to visit again when travel becomes easier. I treasure my friendship with this typically resourceful African family, a friendship now spanning fifty-five years.

14. LATER

I COULD NOT OF COURSE leave Africa for good. It had insinuated itself into me. I had left a little of my heart there, and I manage to return from time to time.

My brief consultancy for SBS involved spending several days a week in the small offices of Blue Circle Cement in Caversham which dealt with Cheecolite, of which SBS were the major customer. It was my first long exposure to the workings of a large and bureaucratic company, and it confirmed my view that it was not an environment into which I would fit.

At the end of my six-month consultancy I negotiated, through a contact with extensive connections in Portugal, a new contract. Using SBS's technology, and notionally on their behalf but bearing all the financial responsibility myself, I would build houses for refugees returning to their motherland when Angola and Mozambique were granted their independence. I took on several of the expatriates with whom I had worked at Kilombero and had a hugely enjoyable nine months, spending one week each month in Lisbon. This came to an abrupt end when my Angolan joint-venture partner embezzled all the funds. I then set up a financial consultancy advising British expatriates on their personal finances, which ensured that I had occasional trips back to sub-Saharan Africa.

A year or so after we left Kenya, we arranged for our house girl Mary to stay with us in Farnham, with a view to her eventually living with us for a couple of years as our au pair. During her visit we all drove down to Lisbon, taking the ferry from Southampton to Santander. Mary had of course seen the sea many times on our visits to the Kenya coast, but this was her first time on board a ship. After we had settled ourselves into our cabin, I took her up on deck. We stood by the railing as she looked in wonder at the sister ship birthed next door, and asked me if our ship was as big as that one. When I told her it was, she asked, in amazement, 'And can it float?'

It was a thirty-six-hour journey and Mary spent much of the day, as we crossed the bay of Biscay, patrolling the decks, constantly looking out over the ocean and obviously nervous. She recovered her usual good humour as soon as we reached Santander and greatly enjoyed the experience of driving through Spain and Portugal. We stopped for the night in Salamanca and asked a policeman the way to the hotel we had chosen. He spoke no English and we struggled with our rudimentary Spanish but eventually got the information we needed. Mary gave a great peal of laughter and said, 'That is another story for the book.' I believe it was the first time she had realised that Europeans could not automatically communicate with each other.

She eventually came to live with us in Farnham, after I had overcome the appalling racism in the Home Office and the British High Commission in Nairobi. At the time, au pair girls came to the UK from continental Europe in their thousands to improve their English, and were granted visas almost automatically. When I applied for a visa for this young woman from Kenya, a one-time British colony and a respected member of what was then still the British Commonwealth, I was told she would have to be interviewed at the British High Commission, an intimidating experience for an uneducated young African woman. Fortunately I had reason to visit Nairobi, so I accompanied her to the interview. At the conclusion the interviewer, an English woman, who very plainly disapproved of the idea of a house servant living as an au pair in the UK, told me that in her opinion Mary spoke perfectly adequate English and therefore would not be granted a visa. I argued that Mary's English was considerably worse than my Danish wife's had been when she herself became an au pair years before. Very reluctantly the visa was issued, and Mary subsequently spent a couple of happy years with us.

Another friend from Africa came to live in Farnham, a move which ended tragically. Some years after we returned to the UK Jim Noon, a keen rally driver, had a car accident leaving him so damaged that he was no longer able to renew his pilot's licence. He moved to the UK, choosing to live in Farnham partly because we were there, became a driving instructor and taught both Marina and Margaret to drive. Trading the left-hand seat of a Cessna 210 flying over the plains of East Africa for the left-hand seat of a small family saloon teaching teenagers to drive in Surrey was, understandably deeply depressing for him; his marriage to Louise broke up and he died young in a house fire, caused by him smoking in bed.

Africa has continued to add charm and interest to my life. On one a visit back to Kenya, staying at the Panafric hotel in Nairobi, I was standing by the restaurant entrance waiting to be allocated a table for breakfast. There was the usual pedestal to give the restaurant manager an illusory air of authority. Before attending to me, he pulled open a drawer and spent a few seconds quietly contemplating its contents. I followed his gaze and saw, sitting in the drawer, a full breakfast on a plate. Expressionless, he closed the drawer and showed me to my table. One of the little unexplained mysteries of life in Africa.

On another trip I found myself in Kitwe on the Zambian copper-belt one Saturday morning with nothing to do. In my visits to the Gulf, weekends were as much part of my work routine as any other days but in Africa I took time off. It was a typical East African morning, sunny and pleasantly warm and

I decided to indulge myself and visit the market. During my years in Kenya I had come to enjoy markets, the colour, the smell, the bustle of people going about life, buying basic foods for their families, gossiping, jostling each other, unworried by the proximity of others. Kitwe was different. There were no tourists on the copper-belt and therefore no stalls selling tourist tat, which sadly has become ubiquitous now. On offer was food, second-hand clothing, cheap goods for everyday life and housewares, cigarettes, fizzy drinks in garish colours, sweets and biscuits – the affordable luxuries enjoyed by small-town Africans.

By that time most of my travel was to Saudi Arabia and the Gulf, where crime was almost non-existent, and I had become casual in my approach to personal safety. In common with most men in the Gulf at that time I carried my valuables, passport, cash and air tickets in a small leather handbag and I had, without thinking, taken it with me to the market. I was enjoying being in a crowd, outside my everyday life of quiet offices, when I became aware that the crowd appeared not to be enjoying me. It abruptly melted away but for three young men, probably no more than teenagers, advancing on me from different directions, eyeing my handbag. To this day I have no idea what prompted me to adopt a karate pose, hands raised into the chopping position, rotate slowly on the ball of my left foot and shout, loud and staccato, 'Hi! Hi! Hi!' It was some atavistic instinct quite foreign to an itinerant accountant, but I did it, and the young men melted back into the crowd. Before they could regroup I scuttled back to the nearby hotel and sluiced the adrenalin away with a couple of beers. A close shave, as they say.

I have had a couple of other handbag incidents. A few years after my visit to Zambia I was in Kuwait staying with my sister Tina. She and her husband Jim went sailing at weekends in their boat, Ibn Battuta, named after the Moroccan explorer and scholar who travelled far more extensively than Marco Polo but is hardly known in the West. One Friday a group of us sailed down the coast for lunch at the beach house of a wealth Kuwaiti. We anchored offshore and went in to the beach in the small tenders which each yacht had in tow. I had with me, of course, my handbag containing my passport, return air ticket and cash. The lunch was accompanied by copious amounts of alcohol – it is a paradox that expatriates seem to drink more where alcohol is forbidden than they do in more tolerant countries – and when it was time to go we boarded the little boats with their outboard motors and headed back to sea.

Ours was aluminium with no built-in buoyancy, the sea was choppy and we began to ship water. We were in the happy stage of inebriation and thought it hilarious when the boat sank beneath us; the sea was warm and we swam the few remaining yards to Ibn Battuta, hauled ourselves on board and fell laughing into the cockpit. I stopped laughing when I realised that my handbag had gone, with the tender, to the bottom of the sea.

Some years later I was in Tirana, walking back to my hotel with a couple of colleagues, having had dinner at one of the very few restaurants which existed in the Albanian capital at the time. I had my handbag tucked under my arm, street lighting was almost non-existent, we stopped to look at something and the bag was suddenly tugged from me. I spun round and gave chase, but I was fifty and he was a teenager. My colleagues told me that I almost caught him, no doubt powered by adrenalin, but he disappeared into the night. Sadly the bag contained a silver Tiffany pen which had been used at an impressive signing ceremony, one of the few mementoes I had from my time as an investment banker. As they say, you never learn: I'm happy that shortly after, such men's handbags went out of fashion.

A few days after the Zambian incident another interesting market visit almost happened. I was back in Lusaka on my last evening before returning to the UK and I decided to try to buy some pot, banghi as it was known in East Africa. I thought about where to find it and decided the simplest and most discrete way was to ask a taxi driver. The conversation sticks in my mind:

'Where can I buy some *banghi?*'

'How much do you want?'

'Just one bag.' I was thinking of the small paper bags we used to buy in the Nairobi chicken market.

'We'll have to go to the big market. It's about twenty kilometres – that okay?'

Taxis weren't expensive and the dope would be cheap so I said, 'Fine.'

A pause. 'You want a bag of *banghi?*'

'That's right.'

Another pause. 'You want one fifty-pound bag of banghi?'

As I was flying back to London the next day, I opted for the alternative he suggested, a couple of ready-rolled joints in a local nightclub. The thought of trying to get on a British Airways plane with a large gunny sack reeking of pot still makes me smile.

When I was back in the UK, I decided to confess to my mother that, during my years in Africa, I had smoked pot (even as adults we sometimes feel the need to confess sins to our mothers). As I endeavoured to tell her without using slang which I thought she might not understand, she interrupted.

'Ah yes,' she said, 'we used to call them reefers.'

What was risqué and illegal to my enlightened post-war generation was simply slightly bohemian to hers.

By the time we left Kenya in 1976 William Ireri was nearly

13 and we promised to keep in touch. He had become almost part of our family, visiting often and acquiring the now long-forgotten nickname of 'pancakes' as he was particularly partial to them - to this day he blames me for his very zany sense of humour. I undertook to give him some financial support while he was at Barnado's, which I did by sending money to a camera shop so that he could buy films and accessories, photography having become his hobby and eventually a modest source of income. In 1988 he came to the UK for his tertiary education at design college and apart from a visit back to Kenya a few years later he has been here ever since, supporting himself and generally contributing to society. I am proud of him.

There was a long period, nearly twenty years, when I didn't visit East Africa. My life was busy and full, and my appetite for travel was sated by regular work trips to the Caribbean and Eastern Europe, and holidays on Indian Ocean islands. Then, in 2010, my brief assignment for the NGO Africa First took me back there. Although Nairobi had changed almost beyond recognition, I was reminded over and over just why I love it. The warmth of the weather and the people, the bustle and laughter, the red earth and the mauve jacarandas, the soaring birds – memories which once more draw me back again and again. As I write this under Covid restrictions I haven't been for nearly two years, but I have every intention of continuing to visit for as long as I am able to travel.

I look back now and know that Africa played a major part in making me what I am. I grew up wanting to be, at various times, an engineer, a merchant banker and a ship-owner, ambitions which grew out of my reading, all based on slightly swash-buckling real or fictitious role models from an earlier era: Weetman Pearson, the first Lord Cowdray, for engineering; the Fleming and Baring families for merchant banking; and the heroes of some of Hammond Innes novels for ship-owning.

I was of course quite unqualified to emulate any of these men or follow any of those career paths (although I did have a brief few years as an investment banker, as unrewarding as it was remunerative). Instead, armed with the confidence which Africa gave me, I did my own thing, which took me, in the course of the rest of my working life, from Barbados to Bahrain, from Moscow to Manila and from Anguilla to Ascension Island; saw me acting as Director of Tourism in one small British Overseas Territory and Commercial Advisor to the government of another; and equipped me to help restore the fortunes of a dying family business.

ACKNOWLEDGEMENTS

First and foremost, thank you to Kenya, for being the amazing country it is. Thank you to the many Kenyans who contributed to the life-changing experiences I had during the years I spent living in their country, particularly the Gathirwa family who remain among my special friends.

Thank you to those who bought copies of my first two books *An Accidental Bookseller* and *An Accidental Envoy* and encouraged me to carry on writing.

A very special thank you to Flora Rees, who edited my draft so brilliantly; I cannot praise her contributions to the finished version highly enough.

Thanks to Jamie Keenan for the design of the book, both the cover and layout. As with my Foyles and Turks and Caicos memoirs his cover has captured some of the essence of my time in Kenya.

Thank you to Assistant Professor Hemath Kumar of National College, Trichy, Tamil Nadu for copy-editing my drafts. As a retired bookseller I understand why Foyles' best-selling book on English grammar is published in India.

Huge thanks to my artist sister-in-law Kim Wordley who surprised me recently with the portrait which appears on the back cover.

And lastly thanks to my wife Vivienne, for her constant encouragement and her critical editing. It is, as I have said before, a great joy to have a wife and partner who shares my passions, including my love of words and of travel.

www.ingramcontent.com/pod-product-compliance
Lightning Source LLC
Chambersburg PA
CBHW06205228042
43661CB00088B/734